JEFFERSON'S PILLOW

Jefferson's Pillow

The Founding Fathers
and the Dilemma of Black Patriotism

ROGER WILKINS

Beacon Press

BOSTON

Beacon Press
25 Beacon Street
Boston, Massachusetts 02108-2892
www.beacon.org

Beacon Press books
are published under the auspices of
the Unitarian Universalist Association of Congregations.

05 04 03 02 01   8 7 6 5 4 3

This book is printed on acid-free paper that meets the uncoated paper
ANSI/NISO specifications for permanence as revised in 1992.

Text design by Elizabeth Elsas
Composition by Wilsted & Taylor Publishing Services

Library of Congress Cataloging-in-Publication Data
Wilkins, Roger W.
    Jefferson's pillow: the founding fathers and the dilemma of Black
    patriotism / Roger Wilkins.
        p. cm.
    Includes bibliographical references and index.
    ISBN 0-8070-0956-3 (acid-free paper)
        1. Statesmen—United States—History—18th century.
    2. Presidents—United States—History—18th Century.   3. Mason,
    George, 1725–1792—Relations with African Americans.   4. Washington,
    George, 1732–1799—Relations with African Americans.   5. Jefferson,
    Thomas, 1743–1826—Relations with African Americans.   6. Madison,
    James, 1751–1836—Relations with African Americans.   7. African
    Americans—Civil rights—History.   8. Nationalism—United States—
    Psychological aspects.   9. Wilkins, Roger W., date.   10. Wilkins family.
    I. Title.

E302.5 . W68 2001
973'.09'9—dc21   2001025117

FOR
PATRICIA AND ELIZABETH

CONTENTS

The past is never dead; in fact, it's not even past.

William Faulkner

And as the moon rose higher the inessential houses began to melt away until gradually I became aware of the old island here that flowered once for Dutch sailors' eyes—a fresh green breast of the new world. Its vanished trees, the trees that had made way for Gatsby's house, had once pandered in whispers to the last and greatest of all human dreams; for a transitory enchanted moment man must have held his breath in the presence of this continent, compelled into an aesthetic contemplation he neither understood nor desired, face to face for the last time in history with something commensurate to his capacity for wonder. . . .

Gatsby believed in the green light, the orgastic future that year by year recedes before us. It eluded us then, but that's no matter—tomorrow we will run faster, stretch out our arms farther. . . . And one fine morning—

So we beat on, boats against the current, borne back ceaselessly into the past.

F. Scott Fitzgerald

"That don't sound like you, Ella. Me and you been pulling colored folk out the water more'n twenty years. Now you tell me you can't offer a man a bed? . . . "

"He ask, I give him anything."

"Why's that necessary all of a sudden?"

"I don't know him all that well."

"You know he's colored."

Toni Morrison

Less than a mile from my home in Washington, on a little penin-
sula jutting out into the Tidal Basin, inside a neoclassical temple,
there is an awesome statue of Thomas Jefferson. He is on a high
pedestal, standing easily and tall in a long coat with a gaze that
seems fixed somewhere far beyond tomorrow. Some of Jefferson's
most memorable words are set in the great stone panels that sur-
round the statue. They are the throbbing phrases at the core of the
American hymn to freedom that Jefferson composed and flung
out against the sky. These are words that have enlarged the hearts
and emboldened the spirits of generations of freedom-loving
people across the globe.

In the thirty-eight years I have lived in Washington, I have visited that place many times—to see it for myself, to show it to my
children, or to show it to visitors who have come from far away.
In the process of writing this book, I decided to visit the memorial again. I am always moved by it because the words touch the
chords of myth and memory that are embedded in the hearts of
most Americans. Who cannot be stirred when he thinks of an
eighteenth-century American who could proclaim to the world:

> We hold these truths to be self-evident; that all men are created equal;
> that they are endowed by their Creator with certain inalienable
> rights; that among these are life, liberty, and the pursuit of happiness;
> that to secure these rights, governments are instituted among men,
> deriving their just powers from the consent of the governed. We . . .
> solemnly publish and declare that these colonies are and of right
> ought to be free and independent states . . . and for the support of this
> declaration, with a firm reliance on the protection of divine provi-
> dence, we mutually pledge our lives, our fortunes and our sacred
> honor.

Or this:

> God who gave us life gave us liberty, can the liberties of a nation be
> secure when we have removed a conviction that these liberties are the
> gift of God? Indeed I tremble for my country when I reflect that God
> is just, that his justice cannot sleep forever. Commerce between Mas-
> ter and slave is despotism. Nothing is more certainly written in the

book of fate than that these people are to be free. Establish the law for educating the common people. This is the business of the state to effect and on a general plan.

Another panel reads:

I am not an advocate for frequent changes in laws and Constitutions. But laws must and institutions must go hand in hand with the progress of the human mind. As that becomes more developed, more enlightened as new discoveries are made, new truths discovered and manners and opinions change, with the change of circumstances, institutions must advance also to keep pace with the times. We might as well require a man to wear still the coat which fitted him when a boy as civilized society to remain ever under the regimen of their barbarous ancestors.

I can feel these ideas pulsing beneath the words of the Supreme Court opinion in the landmark case *Brown v. Board of Education,* in which it reversed its earlier approval of segregation. When Chief Justice Earl Warren wrote to explain the Court's decision, he said:

In approaching this problem, we cannot turn the clock back to 1868 when the [14th] Amendment was written. We must consider public education in the light of its full development and its present place in American life throughout the Nation. Only in this way can it be determined if segregation in public schools deprives these plaintiffs of the equal protection of the laws. . . .

Whatever may have been the extent of psychological knowledge at the time of *Plessy v. Ferguson,* this finding [that segregation has a tendency to retard the educational and mental development of Negro children] is amply supported by modern authority. Any language in *Plessy v. Ferguson* contrary to this finding is rejected.

There is also a panel on the wall of the temple with quotes relating to the issue of religious freedom, and then up high, just before the domed ceiling begins, there is a band with words carved in block capitals: "I HAVE SWORN UPON THE ALTAR OF GOD ETERNAL HOSTILITY AGAINST EVERY FORM OF TYRANNY OVER THE MIND OF MAN."

It is a late-fall afternoon, and the chill has created an atmosphere suited to quiet contemplation because most tourists have chosen warmer destinations. I am standing in a temple of freedom dedicated to enshrining the memory of Thomas Jefferson in those chambers of our hearts reserved for the greatest of human spirits. And yet I am puzzled as I stare up at the image of this man who wrote that his earliest memory was of being carried on a pillow by a slave riding on horseback, and who at the time of his death still owned well over a hundred human beings upon whom, somehow, he had been unwilling or unable to bestow the blessings of liberty.

As I stand alone, notebook in hand, pondering my question, I finally notice that another visitor, a white man, whom I have vaguely sensed circling the statue and therefore me, is staring not at Jefferson's image but at my demeanor as he makes his rounds. It seems that my deep contemplation of Jefferson puzzles him. At this point I notice that, as is often the case, I am the only black person in the temple. A little later on another stranger—also a white man—surreptitiously takes my picture as I stand there trying to understand the expression the sculptor gave to Jefferson's face. Is it *my* expression or my skin color that fascinates these men? Maybe they are asking themselves why I am here. Given all of my experience and all I know of American history, so am I.

On another night, there is another puzzle. This time I am alone in a room in my house watching an Arts and Entertainment Channel movie about Washington's crossing of the Delaware on Christmas Night 1776, and the ensuing battle of Trenton. It is an enthralling drama about the fragility of the dispirited American army and the heroism of the commander in chief, who is depicted as *willing* the army to move, to strike, and to win. It, like the Jefferson Memorial and much else in monumental Washington, is designed to evoke awe and reverence at the contemplation of the founding of the republic and the people who accomplished it. Although I find the film and the valiant struggle it seeks to represent deeply moving, I get an eerie feeling about this version of history. There are no blacks in it. There are no black civilians, no black soldiers, and no black slaves or body servants—just white people bravely and busily creating a country.

Both of these iconic references to the birth of the republic create awful absences in me. Jefferson's utterances on freedom and
liberty are like the neutron bombs of words. They pack terrific
force, but they seem not to have affected very many eighteenth-
century black lives. And the battle of Trenton (and by implication,
the entire Revolution), as rendered by A&E, indicates that blacks
were absent at the creation—a suggestion implicit in most of the
ways that history has been taught for most of the nearly four hundred years America has been making history.

Yet I am always acutely aware that however noble their ac-
complishments, Jefferson and his fellow Virginians George Washington, George Mason, and James Madison—great patriots and
founders all—lived lives cushioned by slavery. They were also the
conveyors of the culture that has done and continues to do hideous damage to millions of black human beings and to many more
millions of white Americans as well. They created a nation conceived in liberty and dedicated to the proposition that whites were
and should be supreme. They celebrated freedom while stealing
the substance of life from the people they "owned." They fought
off the mightiest military power then on earth with the cry "We
will not be slaves!" And they created the country that gives me,
the descendant of slaves and slave owners, much of the context for
my existence, the freedom that I cherish and the democratic citizenship that I have used relentlessly for the past half century.

How is one to understand a country whose dreams the slave
owners despoiled even as they were creating it? How is a black person to regard a land where his ancestors were meant to serve but
not to grow?

As I contemplate the tall, straight figure of Jefferson and think
of his colleagues, I am truly in awe of the conundrum they present
to me and people like me, and of the deep conflict they have laid
on my soul—the "twoness," as W. E. B. Du Bois called it. Because
I am black, I can't avoid it, and because I am American, I must con-
front it. As the new century begins, I am living out my sixty-ninth
year in comfort, with the wonderful and successful wife of my
later years, and my three children are all doing well. I saw Satchel
Paige pitch way back down in Segregation, and I loved him; heard

Frank Sinatra sing and Miles Davis play his horn; inhaled Harlem as a child; fell in love in Ann Arbor and married young in Cleveland; and have spent a lifetime in democratic struggles since then. When I am abroad, I *feel* profoundly American, and I must look that way, too. On a trip to South Africa in 1978, while that nation was still mired in apartheid, I was dressed casually and standing quietly alone, on a street corner in downtown Capetown, waiting to cross. I thought my brown skin made me look very much like the people then classified as "colored" in that country, but before the light changed, a little white South African woman squinted up at my face and asked, "Where're you from, Philadelphia?"

Well, not Philadelphia, but my blood came down through Kansas City, Minneapolis/St. Paul, St. Louis; Pike County, Ohio; Holly Springs, Mississippi; Charleston, South Carolina; Northumberland County, Virginia; and surely a lot of other American places as well. And on that day, on that street corner in Capetown, the gaze of that little white South African woman caught that. Generations of my family are buried in this American ground, and this country has made its mark on us just as we have made our marks on it. My people and I have worked for America, and we have changed it, made it richer and better. The question is whether we blacks can join other Americans—including more recent immigrants—and become the full emotional and civic owners of the place where we were once owned. There is much pain and loss in our national history, which contains powerful echoes of the pain and loss many of us feel in our daily lives. For blacks there is the pain of slavery and the continual loss of dignity that accompanies our treatment as nonstandard citizens. For many Southern whites, the outcome of the Civil War brought a loss of prestige, power, and privilege, and some of the resulting resentment was felt in the North as well. Black people and white people became for each other color-coded symbols of the things they had lost or never achieved, and of the things they continued to resent and fear.

Ancient pains are summoned up to cloak contemporary arguments in the self-righteousness of victimhood. So we divide up our past and use simplistic bits selectively—avoiding real human complexity—in order to fuel the argument of the moment or to meet urgent but unrelated needs. But in so dividing and simplifying history—for example, maintaining that the Confederate flag is merely the symbol of past honor and gallantry or that all blacks were innocent and noble victims—we ensure that our future will be rent along the same jagged seams that wound us so grievously today.

Tales of the republic's founding—mythic national memories used to bind us together—are often told in ways that exclude and diminish all of us. They diminish the founders by denying them rich human complexity and giving us instead monumental heroes whose actual lives cannot possibly live up to the marble facades that have come down to us through the generations; and they diminish blacks either by simply excluding us or by minimizing our humanity and our contributions to the richness, strength, and vibrancy of the nation. And yet I feel and look American, and I have labored over the years to make the Constitution work for everyone. Does that make me a patriot? Can I embrace founders who may have "owned" some of my ancestors? Can I try to see them in their complexity and understand them—even identify with them? Can I see myself and my ancestors as active participants in a history from which we are too often absent?

Perhaps the best way for me to unravel these questions is to look back at the story of the founding and at the characters and achievements of four of the Virginians—George Mason, George Washington, Thomas Jefferson, and James Madison—who were both massive contributors to the founding of the new nation and owners of slaves. The idea of this project is not to write yet another biography of any of these men or another colonial or revolutionary history. It is, rather, to apply what I know as a man who is now a few months older than Washington was when he died—a man who is American, black, and acutely aware of the frailties of humans, himself included. In my effort to understand and to evaluate these men, the revolution they helped make, and the legacy of their entire generation, I will try very hard to remember the constraints that culture imposes on free will. I will try to discern how they accepted or endeavored to reform their society, and look again at how they performed at some of the most challenging moments of their lives. I will probe their cultural and intellectual inheritance so as to avoid judging them by contemporary values—as my older daughter, Amy, judged George Washington when she was a little girl and learned on a visit to Mount Vernon that he had owned slaves.

"What's so great about him?" she exclaimed shrilly.

In the shock and quiet that followed, I didn't answer.

This book is, finally, an attempt at a response.

I often tell my students that we are all born with a thousand pounds of history on our back. This was no less true for the founding generation than it is for us. In an effort to make explicit the basis for my judgments, I will draw the history of the founding, up through what I know of slavery in my own family and then up through my own ruminations on being an American citizen. These latter may have begun in earnest when I was eight and attended my father's burial in a segregated cemetery in Missouri, where, in 1941, blacks were not considered good enough to be around whites even when they were dead.

First, briefly, let me provide sketches of some founders in their time and then some notes on my family, drawing America into my soul as best I can. Notes, as my brother Jimmy Baldwin would have called them, of a Native Son.

CHAPTER I

Tainted Origins

[The Virginia Declaration of Rights, drafted in 1776 by George Mason,] was meant to embrace the case of free citizens, or aliens only; and not to be a side wind to overturn the rights of property, and give freedom to those very people whom we have been compelled from imperious circumstances to retain, generally, in the same state of bondage that they were in at the revolution, in which they had no concern, agency or interest.

> *Hudgins v. Wright,* Hen. and M. 1 Va., 134 (1806),
> Justice St. George Tucker writing for the Virginia Court of Appeals

We Americans normally seek our beginnings in the revolutionary period and in the words and deeds of the founding fathers. Although we may peer a little bit behind the events of the mid-1770s, we usually don't go much further back than the Stamp Act, the Boston Massacre, and then on to Lexington and Concord. But our inspiration and our sense of ourselves as a people come from the work and the thought of people all up and down the eastern seaboard who came to maturity in the middle of the eighteenth century. Among the major sources of our identity are the things that Thomas Jefferson wrote, George Washington did, James Madison conceived and organized, and George Mason drafted and helped force into the Constitution.

Three of these men—Jefferson, author of the Declaration of Independence, Washington, father of the country, and Madison, father of the Constitution—have achieved mythic proportions in our collective story about our national identity. The lesser-known George Mason wrote the Virginia Declaration of Rights, on which the Bill of Rights in our federal Constitution and the bills of rights in most state constitutions are patterned, and he contributed powerfully to the political movement to add the Bill of Rights to the Constitution. He was a charter member of the political and social group to which the other three belonged, and a mentor to all of them, and he should rank with them in our consciousness.

We generally look at these men in the fullness of their lives when we try to understand what our country is and who we are as a people. We rightly think of them and their generation as the original Americans, and often that is enough of an identification for us. But if we are to understand fully who we are, we must probe more deeply into who these four were by looking at the forces that shaped them, the culture they were heir to, their dreams, insecurities, and fears, the cultural constraints they faced, and finally their growth and their failures as they battled the formal structures of the world they'd inherited.

These four men all entered adulthood having navigated childhood and youth with great success. It might be argued that from birth they enjoyed enormous advantages, but it is surely unarguable that not everyone born to great advantage makes the best use of good fortune. All these men circumvented the pitfalls of indolence, skirt chasing, and gambling that stunted the lives of so many of their contemporaries and of so many young men in every generation who are favored by fortune. Instead, they drove through their early years with enormous determination and a fierce will to extract the maximum out of the extraordinary endowments—both genetic and material—they had received as a birthright.

Along with their gifts, however, these men also inherited a culture and a complete set of assumptions about the world, people, and the natural order of things. However great their gifts and however hard they worked, it was not possible for them to lift themselves out of their time and culture, and it is in that context that they must be judged. As a young man, each of them surely passed the test that one of my great mentors, Justice Thurgood Marshall, said late in his life he would want applied to him.

"I hope they'll say," Marshall told an interviewer, referring to future generations, " 'He did the best he could with what he had.' "

Virginia was the first and largest of the original colonies. In its development were contained many of the most important seeds of our contemporary society. Englishmen first met Native Americans in Virginia and began their systematic decimation of them there. English problems were deposited in Virginia, as were English customs and English ways of understanding the world and organizing society. But ways of being American began to be worked out in Virginia before the idea of America was even developed. American slavery was invented in Virginia, and the yeast of that slave culture contributed significantly to the emerging conceptions of American freedom. Virginians grasped the vastness of the possibility of America, and the conflation of western lands with ideas of the future and of national and personal problem-solving commenced there, too.

I have an additional, more personal reason for wanting to study Virginia: I am descended from a number of old Virginia families. Two branches of my family began with enslaved Virginians, at least as early as the late eighteenth century. Another branch began with members of the Cherokee Nation. We know from family lore and from the appearance of a number of my ancestors that white eighteenth-century slave owners—probably Englishmen —had, at some time in the past, injected themselves into the bloodstreams of the Virginia people I can identify as my great-grandparents.

Although we now think of them as Americans, Washington, Madison, Mason, and Jefferson were actually born Englishmen in a tamed wilderness. They viewed themselves as subjects of the English king, if a particularly testy breed.

Thus, in a letter written to the Committee of London Merchants in June 1766, just under nine years before shots would be fired at Lexington and Concord, George Mason could define himself as

> . . . a man who spends most of his time in retirement, and has seldom med[d]led in public Affairs, who enjoys a moderate but independent Fortune, and content with the Blessings of a private Station, equally disregards the Smiles & Frowns of the Great, who tho not born

> within the Verge of the British Isle, is an Englishman in his Principles, a Zealous Asserter of the Act of Settlement, firmly attached to the present royal Family upon the Throne, unalienably affected to his Majesty's sacred Person & Government, in the Defence of which he wou'd shed the last Drop of his Blood . . . who adores the Wisdom & Happiness of the British Constitution; and if he had his election now to make, wou'd prefer it to any that does, or ever did exist. I am not singular in this my Political Creed; these are the general Principles of his Majesty's Subjects in America. . . .

Just a year after the Stamp Act crisis inflamed the passions of Americans and made them bitter toward Parliament and suspicious of it, the forty-one-year-old Mason could not possibly have been clearer about his loyalty to the British Crown or his devotion to the British Constitution. Earlier in the same letter, he laid out what he valued in his English constitutional heritage:

> Let our fellow-Subjects in Great Britain reflect that we are descended from the same Stock with themselves, nurtured in the same Principles of Freedom; which we have both sucked in with our Mother's Milk: that in crossing the Atlantic Ocean, we have only changed our Climate, not our Minds, our Natures & Dispositions remain unaltered: that We are still the same people with them, in Every Respect; only not yet debauched by Wealth, Luxury, venality, & Corruption. . . .

Mason signed this remarkable missive "A Virginia Planter."

The talents and passions that made Mason a great revolutionary and nation-builder are evident in this letter. In it he refers to the "Passion natural to the mind of Man, especially a free Man, which renders him impatient of Restraint." That, of course, is the passion which, having been activated a year earlier, would be wound tighter and tighter over the course of the ensuing nine years until the rupture of April 1775 would become inevitable.

Thus the proud Mason, who would not be "restrained," was the product and beneficiary of much that had happened on both sides of the Atlantic in the century preceding his birth. The constitutional arrangements securing his British freedoms had been worked out in the English civil wars of the seventeenth century and through the intellectual activity they had generated. Of course, his economic and cultural status as lord of the manor in a slave society had been made possible by the perfection of the systematic international trade in slaves among Africa, Europe, and the Western Hemisphere in the sixteenth and seventeenth centuries, and by the seizure of the economic, political, and cultural high ground in Virginia by his ancestors in the seventeenth century.

All of that came together to make Mason the man he was in 1766, but he was far prouder of his constitutional heritage than he was of the social developments that led him—like his fellow Virginia founders—to be master of his own private penal colony. Thus he, like the others, was far more likely to dwell, in his public utterances, on the writings of Adam Smith and John Locke than on the steps that led from the purchase of twenty blacks by the Jamestown Colony in August 1619—the first recorded arrival of blacks in any part of the territory that would become the thirteen colonies—to his own ownership of and dependence upon scores of human beings in the middle of the eighteenth century.

A document describing events that occurred a decade or so before Mason wrote his letter to the London merchants might be read as a companion to it, an elaboration of the nature of Mason's gentlemanly circumstances. The document is a sliver of Olaudah Equiano's narrative of his enslavement: his description of the day in his childhood, in his home village in a region of what is now Nigeria, when he and his sister were caught in the furthest reaches of the economic machine that sustained Mason and his colleagues. Equiano wrote:

> . . . One day, when all our people were gone out to their work as usual, and only I and my sister were left to mind the house, two men and a woman got over our walls, and in a moment seized us both; and without giving us time to cry out, or to make any resistance, they stopped our mouths and ran off with us into the nearest wood. . . . For a long time we had kept [to] the woods, but at last we came into

a road which I believed I knew. I had now some hopes of being delivered; for we had advanced but a little way before I discovered some
people at a distance, on which I began to cry out for their assistance;
but my cries had no other effect than to make them tie me faster and
stop my mouth; they then put me into a large sack. They also stopped
my sister's mouth and tied her hands.

Equiano and his sister were now beyond the reach of family,
friends, kinsmen, and all familiar places and things. Soon they
would be separated from and deprived of each other forever. They
had been sucked into international commerce and would never
return home again.

Although Mason himself was impatient of "Restraints," it is
doubtful that he would have deployed the same passion for freedom on behalf of young Olaudah that he would deploy for himself and his compatriots. His Englishness, so liberating in some
senses, was severely confining in others. It did leave him open to
the ideas of English and Scots Enlightenment thinkers, but to little else. White Christian Englishness was the only norm of civilization that such men knew or recognized. Other people with
different ways and different cultures could not possibly be understood as anything but inferior.

After all, whatever shackles the seventeenth-century upheav-
als had loosened, the English were still enmeshed in a hierarchical
and patriarchal culture. They could still view the poor *whites* at the
bottom of their society as filth and scum, and limit their awarding
of full citizenship to *men* whose standing derived from substantial
ownership of property—which in Virginia necessarily included
ownership of scores of slaves. Thus, though Mason might have
been troubled by the stark image of two children being kidnapped
just outside their front door, there was nothing in his history or in
his learning that would have persuaded him to extend the protection of his ideas of freedom to those two helpless black children as
they began their journey to the Western Hemisphere.

Not only did the English heritage to which Mason was initially so powerfully attached tolerate the unequal treatment of
human beings; it was built on human inequality. In sixteenth-

century England, where English thrusts across the Atlantic were first fashioned, there was a sharp and clear hierarchy by which to classify white human beings. It flowed from the king down through lesser royalty to landed aristocrats, the clergy, the urban bourgeois, peasant farm laborers, urban laborers, and finally those people with neither rank nor economic purpose.

By the late sixteenth century such people had begun to comprise a growing segment of the British population, thanks to drastic economic changes. Rural peasants found themselves thrown off the land as old agricultural patterns were abandoned and the raising of sheep for wool became a more productive use of the land. So people whose economic utility had ended started roaming the countryside as latter-day hunters and gatherers. Some of them also headed for the cities, where still fewer found economic purpose.

These women and men who had in a sense become little more than social refuse were not socially and politically invisible, however. Rootless, impoverished, and desperate, they were seen as a threat to the social order. The attitudes toward them and the programs devised to solve the problem and "improve" the poor, echoing through the centuries, are stunningly familiar to contemporary black Americans. The condition of the poor was ascribed to their own defects of character. They were deemed lazy, violent, prone to criminality and drunkenness, and hopelessly immoral. Measures were taken to try to put them to work. Enormous efforts were made to stamp out "idleness." Parliament enacted the Statute of Artificers in 1563, which required workmen to labor from five in the morning until seven at night from March to September, and from sunup to sundown the rest of the year.

For those whose idleness was not sopped up by these measures, there were workhouses and poorhouses and prisons. The gallows and the army were other alternatives. But there were still too many idle men for the comfort and emotional well-being of the well-to-do.

The parallel ends here because late-sixteenth- and early-seventeenth-century English policymakers could contemplate options not open to late-twentieth-century Americans. The Portuguese and the Spaniards were by this time colonizing the New World vigorously and accumulating wealth in amounts that threatened to upset the balance of power in Europe. London policymakers saw an opportunity to kill two birds with one stone. People who were viewed as idle, dangerous, or too undisciplined were targeted for export to the New World, where they would be put to work making money for the mother country. They went for the most part as indentured servants, owned usually for seven-year terms, during which they could be bought and sold. Virginia was a rugged place, and many of them were given hard usage. Some visitors to the colony were appalled by how badly these servants were treated.

All in all, Englishmen at the end of the sixteenth century and the beginning of the seventeenth were quite proud of the civilization they had crafted for themselves. John Locke had placed the rights of at least some Englishmen on the firm footing of natural law. He was summing up an enormous national achievement. The English surely viewed themselves as among the most civilized people on earth.

Their early explorations of Africa had confirmed this for them. There they encountered people who were an identifiable and startling "other" in that they were black and non-Christian. Christianity was the essential element of civilization, and whiteness was not simply the Englishman's norm; it was a color packed with symbolism. In his probing history of antiblack racism, Winthrop Jordan has concluded that English culture, in which white stood for purity and beauty, and black for evil and filth, provided clues for the way Englishmen were to regard black human beings—as exotic, "brutal," and "bestial."

Thus, when the English began to collide with people unlike themselves early in the seventeenth century, they already had a handy cultural matrix in which to place those different from themselves. There were hierarchies of human beings, and propertied white English Christians were at the top of the pyramid. Then, during this early period of intercontinental exploration, when the population of the entire world was only about five hundred million, the English came across the Indians, a new people whose skin was not white, black, or yellow and who were not Christians. The categorization of human beings and the assignment of a rank order to them were natural cultural activities for the Englishmen who disembarked at Jamestown in 1607. By the time the first blacks were sold to the colony twelve years later, racial division and mistrust had already become integral features of Virginia life.

Because George Mason's family, and the families of those of his contemporaries who were also members of Virginia's ruling class, had been in Virginia for several generations, they were, for all their somewhat impudent protestations, a special breed of Englishmen. In a sense, they hung suspended between the world from which their ancestors had emigrated and the new world waiting fully to be born. They lived grand lives in Virginia that were modeled after grand lives lived in England, but at the same time they felt keenly that their aspirations to gentility were not sufficiently acknowledged by their English cousins. As a matter of fact, they believed they were objects of scorn, and they hated it. Nowhere was that feeling expressed more colorfully than in the beginning of Mason's letter to the Committee of London Merchants, when he wrote:

> The Epithets of Parent & Child have been so long applyed to Great Britain & her Colonys, that Individuals have adopted them and we rarely see anything, from your Side of the Water, free from the authoritative Style of a Master to a School-Boy.
> "We have, with infinite Difficulty & Fatigue got you excused this one Time; pray be a good boy for the future; do what your Papa and Mamma bid you & hasten to return them your most grateful Acknowledgements for condescending to let you keep what is your own; and then all your Acquaintance will love you, & praise you, & give you pretty things. . . . "

The colonists and their ancestors had forged for themselves the sense of dignity that had been so grievously offended over the century before Mason wrote his letter. It had, in fact, been deeply defined by a rebellion led by Nathaniel Bacon in 1676, nearly seventy years after the first whites arrived in Virginia.

As the last quarter of the seventeenth century opened, the Virginia Colony was still a rugged frontier land, but it was settling down to some extent. Tobacco had become the driving force of the economy; a group of the shrewdest and toughest men had gained control of economic life and a good share of political life as well, but they were still a rough lot, and there were people around who could remember when some of the most powerful had had nothing. For the most part, gaining control of economic life meant assembling land and workers and capital (or credit) enough to do large-scale tobacco farming. The colony, however, was full of landless men who had come over from England as indentured servants, had since served out their terms, and now had neither land nor economic prospects, and whose exploitation for profit thus continued, as they saw it, into their lives as freemen.

The turbulence began in the summer of 1675 in Virginia, when colonists—led by, among others, George Mason's great-grandfather—reacted to an alleged crime by members of one Indian tribe by killing a number of members of another tribe, one that was at peace with the whites. Efforts to quell the trouble failed, so Governor Berkeley proposed building a series of forts to protect the colony. To the landless men of the outlying counties, the measure appeared to be useless as a defense against the Native Americans but highly effective as a means of pouring money into the pockets of the clique around the governor, who would get the bulk of the contracting work on the forts. The noisily expressed resentment of the landless men at those who presumed to rule them began to create a tangible danger. Nathaniel Bacon, a well-connected young man who had come to the colony and been appointed to the governor's council, stepped into the crisis.

Knowing that the grumbling dissenters hated the Native Americans, as he himself did, Bacon counseled the governor to shelve his plan to build expensive and ineffective forts and instead to permit him, Bacon, to lead armed frontiersmen against the Indians. After initial success in a limited foray, Bacon again asked the governor for official authority to conduct his anti–Native American warfare, but Berkeley waffled. Bacon, who now had a fervent band of supporters that included both black and white dispossessed men, proceeded anyway, but now in a different direction: frustrated by the governor's bumbling, he and his men turned their martial attentions from the Native Americans to the elite. During the summer of 1676, they devastated Jamestown and Gloucester County, where the wealthiest of the big Virginia men resided. They burned down Jamestown and plundered the Gloucester County homes of those who they believed had been skimming off the colony's wealth. The governor and his clique were forced to flee with their families.

After only a few months of plunder and pillage, which terrified the ruling class, Bacon fell ill and died. Without its leader, his revolution soon petered out. Although he left no political credo, the events taught powerful lessons on the dangers of class antagonisms within the population. The major men in the colony would work to ensure that their descendants would acquire the education and polished manners necessary to secure the deference of the lower ranks of whites. And more significantly, the elite learned that class consciousness and racial hatred were potent adhesives, capable of creating a coalition that could threaten the existing ruling structure. The elite would subsequently turn racial hatred inward and use it to stifle class conflicts among whites. The power of Bacon's rebellion had sprung from the union of poor blacks and whites against a perceived common enemy; when the Native Americans, at least at home in Virginia, proved too elusive to serve as an effective distraction, the role fell to blacks, whose utility as slaves was already being demonstrated in the colony.

Power would continue to be concentrated in the hands of the wealthy, and the system would be fine-tuned to diminish the number of landless (and therefore dangerous) white men entering the society. These men had proved how hungry and aggressive they could be, and how much of a threat they posed to the social order and to the security of the ruling class. Blacks would now be clearly installed at the bottom rung of the ladder, and what little freedom and few rights they enjoyed would be stripped away. The legislature and the courts began codifying slavery in the laws of the colony, thus sealing the fate of the growing numbers of blacks who began to be imported at the turn of the century. Poor whites could therefore form their identities around their whiteness rather than around their resentments of the rich. Among those involved in the tumultuous events of 1675 and 1676, and absorbing these lessons, were Colonel Mason and Colonel John Washington, ancestors of George Mason and George Washington, and William Byrd, father of William Byrd II, who would become a virtual role model for Virginia's landed gentry in regarding political power as a prime entitlement in the eighteenth century.

Interestingly, just as poor whites were being invited by the lords of the colony to join a sort of white social club, the actual social distance between them and the rich was widening. They would be explicitly reminded of their lower status by the increasing rigidities being constructed into the social system and by the barriers developed to protect the position of holders of power and privilege. As social mobility decreased, personal frustration grew. The rage inspired by the personal suspicion of not being good enough to reach the top—a rage that might otherwise be transformed by a skillful demagogue into rebellious impulses—was now directed at the "others" whose manifest failures were even greater than those of the lower-class whites. Poor whites were thus given two things by the new system: a floor of failure below which they could not fall, and human targets at whom they could direct their own self-loathing. As a result, a persuasive argument could be made that the aftermath of Bacon's rebellion marked the institutionalization of race and racism in the North American culture.

Governor Berkeley and his associates decided to enhance their claim to preeminence in the colony by ensuring that their sons acquired social and intellectual graces that helped rationalize their hold on political power. Practical lessons in the art of living up to the privileges they had inherited began when boys were about five and were placed firmly under the wings of their fathers. They were furnished with smaller versions of grown men's clothes and a slave or two as they were schooled in the ways of their class.

Such fathers tended to their sons' formal education as well. Tutors were imported from the north for the early years, and whenever possible, the young aristocrats were sent to college in England to achieve the ultimate polish. The richest among them also began to build grand manor houses—in the fashion of English country houses—on the banks of Virginia's great rivers.

By 1766, when Mason issued his wail of aggrievement, the dreams of the 1676 generation had been well realized. Although Mason himself had not gone off to college, he had been tutored and given access to his uncle's extensive law library, and he had thus been able to study hard and to read deeply in governmental theory and legal practice. Washington, for his part, had gotten his most valuable education in the saddle, in battle, learning surveying and sleeping under the stars—unlike his two older half-brothers, who had been educated in England. Jefferson obtained his education at William and Mary, and Madison would be educated at the College of New Jersey (now Princeton).

Mason's family was seated at Gunston Hall, and Washington's at Mount Vernon (just a bit up the Potomac from Gunston Hall); Jefferson was raised on his family's plantation at Shadwell, before he climbed his little mountain to build his dream house, and Madison at Montpelier. The policies of 1676 had worked so well over the succeeding century that one of Jefferson's principal biographers could assert that in Jefferson's generation of Virginians, wealth and power were "riveted" together. And wealth and power, together with the status and the grand feelings of mastery that went with them, all rested on the foundation of slavery.

As the seventeenth century ended, the importation of blacks surged, and with it the concern of the planter class over control of blacks. When Bacon waged his rebellion, there were only a few thousand blacks in Virginia, but twenty-four years later they were beginning to outnumber white servants. By the time of the Revolution, 40 percent of all Virginians were black. Slavery depended on violence, and as the economic and psychological dependence upon slavery grew, Virginians began enshrining more and more violence against them in the laws of the colony. In 1680, just four years after Bacon's Rebellion, the House of Burgesses (the first elected assembly in North America), began pulling together and codifying the scattered provisions regulating slaves' lives. The 1680 law is instructive about the intent of the rulers:

> Act X. Whereas the frequent meetings of considerable numbers of Negro slaves under pretense of feasts and burials is judged of dangerous consequence [it is] enacted that no Negro or slave may carry arms, such as any club, staff, gun, sword, or other weapon, nor go from his owner's plantation without a certificate and then only on necessary occasions; the punishment twenty lashes on the bare back, well laid on. And further, if any Negro lift up his hand against any Christian he shall receive thirty lashes, and if he absent himself or lie out from his master's service and resist lawful apprehension, he may be killed and this *law* shall be published every six months.

The respective perceptions, experiences, and expectations of master and slave were fundamentally at odds. The slaves knew they were fully human, but the masters convinced themselves otherwise. While the masters wanted the slaves to serve as technology—perfect and seamless extensions of their will, and precise, cheap, and efficient means of production—the slaves wanted some acknowledgment of their humanity, the freedom to choose their own lives, and spiritual and living space without the threat of beatings and other forms of coercion. The masters demanded absolute obedience; the slaves devised every means possible within the narrow sphere available to them to resist and create lives for themselves. Masters had force, control of culture and politics, and economic power. Slaves had their humanity, guile, whatever courage they could muster, and, ultimately, the power of self-destruction. The fundamental arbiter of these differences was always violence or the threat of it.

The masters' inability to impose their will absolutely on the slaves, their annoyance at the inefficient production that resulted from slaves' passive resistance, and their fear that slaves might seek violent retribution for the wrongs that somewhere deep down the masters knew they were doing were constant subjects of slave-owner discourse—a discourse that found expression in obsessive legislative fretting. Reviewing this period, Judge Leon Higgenbotham noted that "by 1705 Virginia had rationalized, codified, and judicially affirmed its exclusion of blacks from any basic concept of human rights under the law. After the 1705 slave code, Virginia made several revisions, in acts passed in 1710, 1723, 1726, 1727, 1732, 1744, 1748, 1753, 1765, 1769, 1778, 1782, 1785, 1787, 1789, and 1792. The 1792 act was the last and most comprehensive codification of the slave codes in eighteenth-century Virginia. Yet, from 1705 to 1792 there was no change of substantial significance to improve the status of slaves or free blacks."

Sometimes, however, even laws were not enough. During the early decades of the 1700s, when the volume of importations was at its peak for the century, some owners found it expedient to "season" newly imported Africans. It was a relatively standard practice for slave owner to maim a reluctant slave now and then, ordering one of his overseers to lop off a toe, a finger, or an ear of such a fellow to make sure he got the basic ideas: what he was there for and who was boss.

But it would be wrong to suggest that the life of a plantation slave owner was simply unalloyed worry, anxiety, concern, and travail created by the ownership of slaves. William Byrd II of Westover was emblematic of the planter generation that came between Bacon's Rebellion and Mason. Byrd's father had briefly joined Bacon but then had nimbly changed sides and gone on to found a great landed dynasty. He sent his son to study law in London, and once there, young Byrd tried mightily, but unsuccessfully, to marry money and status. Rebuffed in that and in other efforts to insinuate himself into the highest ranks of English society, young Byrd went home and entered into Virginia politics. He sought for a time the prestige of the king's designation as governor of Virginia; failing that, he joined in an attempt to diminish the authority of the king's council in the colony, ultimately returning to London to serve as the agent for colonial resistance to the king's authority.

Whereas William Byrd had fought ruthlessly for power and position in Virginia, his son's aspirations were schizophrenic. He yearned for acceptance in the highest circles in London, but he also sought to be his countrymen's champion. That struggle in the psyche of Byrd II in the early decades of the eighteenth century was to be replicated in many other Virginia souls and then in souls throughout the colonies as the decades wore on. And those personal struggles would run together with those that tens of thousands of others were having in their individual ways, and all would inform the politics of the colonies in the 1760s and 1770s.

But resistance to the king's authority was not limited to Byrd II or the king's council. As a matter of fact, they were late and timid compared to the House of Burgesses. Less than a century after its creation, the assembly embarked on the long path of colonial resistance to English authority. Byrd II's plots to supplant the governor took form in the 1720s, but the burgesses had begun resisting him on a broader front as early as 1714. When Byrd II's maneuvers were ultimately rejected by England, he lowered his sights and brought his fancy English education and English gentility into harness with the politics of the burgesses as they forged new paths for Virginia.

Landon Carter, another second-generation Virginia gentry man, was born in 1710, when Byrd II was thirty-six. He, too, was part of the transitional generation and was sent to England for education for roughly the same reasons as Byrd. After that, Carter was never quite comfortable back home in the role of the provincial. Both of these men suffered something akin to the problems encountered by the bright barrio or ghetto youngster who is selected and groomed and sent to Harvard and then tries to return to his or her roots. According to Kenneth A. Lockridge, Landon Carter "adapted the new English model of the gentleman as enlightened agriculturalist, creating a subrole which was to become a part of the model for all gentlemen in Virginia as well." Carter—perhaps because of the conflicts inherent in his having to be one of the carriers of the English model gentry into a maturing Virginia—was a brittle man who couldn't stand his own imperfections and thus hid from public scrutiny.

When William Byrd II finally gave up his dream of a king's appointment to certify his gentility, he settled more comfortably into life in Virginia. His newfound comfort, coupled with a continuing need to convince his English friends of the quality of Virginia gentry, may have prompted Byrd II to describe his life this way in the late 1720s in a letter to an English friend:

> Like one of the patriarchs of old, I have my flocks and my herds, my bond-men and bond-women, and every soart of trade amongst my own servants, so that I live in a kind of independence on every one, but Providence. However, tho' this soart of life is without expense yet it is attended with a great deal of trouble. I must take care to keep all my people to their duty, to set all the springs in motion, and to make every one draw his equal share to carry the machine forward. But then 'tis an amusement in this silent country, and a continual exercise of our patience and economy.
>
> . . . Another thing my Lord, that recommends this country much, we sit securely under our vines, and our fig trees without any danger to our property. We have neither publick robbers nor private, which your Lordship will think very strange when we have needy governours, and pilfering convicts sent over among us. . . .

There is surely a large element of "So there," in the letter. He is basically saying, "I don't need England, her corruption and fancy women, her haughty airs, or any of the other things that English rejection of me as a provincial denied to me. Life is sweet here, and safe. We may be provincial, but we are lords in our own right and surely not servile. We have, on the one hand, pushed back authority sufficiently to give us ample space to be grand gentlemen and, on the other, found ways to contain or pacify the rabble so that we have an orderly and predictable community."

But certainly there was also a great deal of truth to Byrd's nose-thumbing. His diaries show that he did find a great deal of quiet enjoyment under his vines and his fig trees, and that he had reached as reasonable an accommodation with "his people" as one managing an operation burdened by hereditary chattel slavery could hope for. There were, to be sure, annoyances rooted in the decisions and the policies of the mother country. There were the convicts sent over to populate the colony, and the Englishmen who were not "secured," like the governor, and who could and presumably did "bite [and] tear" the colonists from time to time. Thus the strains in the transatlantic relationship endured.

Nevertheless, the colony was stable, and the governorship had been tamed to some degree. Byrd was a rich and powerful man with several plantations, and he was living a very good life. The class of Virginians he lived among and was describing just at the time of Mason's birth was the class into which Mason and after him Washington, Jefferson, and Madison would be born. That generation would inherit the life, the proud attitudes, the property—including human chattel—and the resentments of the man who boasted of living "like one of the patriarchs of old." All of this was evident in Mason's letter to the London merchants, and it would profoundly inform revolutionary politics in Virginia.

In mid-June 1776, Colonel George Mason of Gunston Hall finished his work as leader of the committee that had been charged by the Virginia Convention in Williamsburg with preparing a "DECLARATION OF RIGHTS, and such a plan of government as will be most likely to maintain peace and order in this colony, and secure substantial and equal liberty to the people"—the major formal step in the emergence from colonial status of an independent Virginia. The first sentence of his proposed Declaration of Rights for Virginians asserted "that all men are by nature equally free and independent, and have certain inherent rights, of which they cannot by any compact deprive or divest their posterity. . . . "

At the time he wrote these words, Mason was a major Virginia slave owner, having inherited a substantial estate and scores of slaves from his father. He had absorbed from the carefully crafted upper-class culture of Virginia the style and the habits of the patriarch. He ruled as a sovereign over an estate that depended, in virtually all respects, upon the perpetual subordination of the people whose freedom, labor, hope, and natural rights he was stealing. When these people came to Mason with one request or another, they were required to kneel before addressing him.

Given all of that, how could Mason possibly have written such a sentence in earnest? How could he and his colleagues Washington, Jefferson, and Madison, owning among them about four hundred human beings, have struggled so hard, so long, and so effectively under the banner of freedom and liberty? Mason's words pose the question sharply, and the way they came to flower in his mind and the way they were ultimately changed by the Virginia Convention help explain a great deal about how he and the other Virginia founders engaged the issue of human equality.

Virginia life after Bacon's Rebellion offers part of the answer, but other powerful strands of the culture were at work as well. One such factor was a relatively new and exciting intellectual construct that, as Mason's letter to the Committee of London Merchants indicates, shaped his and his peers' sense of who they were and how they fit in the world. Another factor consisted in the deep cultural understandings—particularly about the rank ordering of human beings—that had so grown into the lives of the people that they were accepted uncritically as the way things were and ought to be.

The commanding intellectual construct the founders would ride had gained force in England and Scotland during the course of the English civil war of the mid–seventeenth century, waged just as the strong men who were the great-grandfathers of the founding generation were consolidating their hold on economic and political power across the Atlantic in Virginia. The Cromwell revolution stirred ideas of limited monarchy, parliamentary superiority, and greater accountability both of Parliament to the people and of the national executive to the Parliament. All of these ideas were to become political reality in 1688 with the Glorious Revolution, which would install William and Mary on the throne.

There were great debates in England, however, about where sovereignty actually lay, and over opposing theories of parliamentary representation. Although the Cromwell era was of short duration, the ideas debated during the period of his commonwealth were to have great resonance 125 years later in the seaboard colonies of North America. Mainstream Commonwealthmen —the Independents—maintained that representation in Parliament should depend on property ownership. They wanted the parliamentary seats redistributed, away from those holding them by hereditary right and toward constituencies of taxpayers. Cromwell's son-in-law Henry Ireton, a leading spokesman for the Independents, held that the right to vote rested on a "permanent fixed interest in the Kingdom." He believed that property owners had a vested interest because "he that hath his livelihood by his trade, and by his freedom of trading in such a corporation, which he cannot exercise in another, he is tied to that place, [for] his livelihood depends upon it. And, secondly, that man hath an interest, hath a permanent interest there, upon which he may live, and live a freeman without dependence." That position was only a limited modification of the traditional view of parliamentary representation in England and would be compatible with voting qualifications carried into the early stages of the American republic.

The mainstream Commonwealthmen were opposed by a group of lower-ranking soldiers, the Levellers, whose ideas of reform, sovereignty, and representation were more radical. Although recent scholarship has suggested that the Levellers in fact believed political rights were due only to free, non-wage-earning men, their rhetoric seems to foreshadow sentiments that contemporary Americans like to attribute to their own nation's founders. Major William Rainborough, a principal Leveller leader, expressed it this way:

> I think that the poorest he that is in England hath a life to live, as the greatest he; and therefore truly sir I think it is clear that every man that is to live under a government ought first by his own consent to put himself under that government; and I do think that the poorest man in England is not at all bound in a strict sense to that government that he hath not had a voice to put himself under; and I am confident that, when I have heard the reasons against it, something will be said to answer those reasons, insomuch that I should doubt whether he was an Englishman or no that should doubt of these things.

Here Rainborough surely seems to be saying that all men are created equal, and that since governments rule legitimately only by the consent of the governed, *all* men have a right to vote for Parliament without regard to their property interests, for that vote constitutes their consent.

The writings of many seventeenth- and early-eighteenth-century theorists in England and Scotland and on the European continent were used as fuel for the burning arguments that moved the colonists toward revolution. Particularly influential in this regard were John Trenchard and Thomas Gordon, two searing and prolific denouncers of the tight group of courtiers and ministers who formed the inner (and, to the critics' minds, corrupt) circle that ruled England. Bernard Baylin has observed that "in America, where they were republished entire or in part again and again[,] . . . the writings of Trenchard and Gordon ranked with the treatises of Locke as the most authoritative statement of the nature of political liberty and above Locke as an exposition of the social sources of the threats it faced."

Ultimately, out of the torrent of intellectual churning that followed the English civil war, Locke's ideas seemed to settle most firmly in the minds of Mason and Jefferson as they made their intellectual contributions to the founding of the new nation. In his "Second Treatise on Government," published in 1690, Locke assumed a national community that endured through changes of government and that had values which the government in power at any given time was required to respect. Beyond that, however, Locke saw "natural law" as imbuing *individuals* with rights that neither society nor government could strip from them. Flowing from moral values, such natural laws were broader than the laws governments enacted, and existed prior to their formation. Locke often spoke of these natural rights as "life, liberty, and estate," though he sometimes cited "property" as well. He elaborated on this last right more than on the others, explaining that by mixing his labor with elements found in nature, man extended himself and made that upon which he labored part of himself. Property, then, seems central to Locke's conception of individuals who had some standing and were deserving of protection from invasion by either government or society. Locke appears to have had no objection to slavery as it was practiced as a matter of property in the English colonies.

George Mason's draft of the Virginia Declaration of Rights centered on Locke's natural-rights theories and on his conception of property-holding as a component of citizenship. Mason borrowed heavily from Locke in asserting "that all men are free and independent, and have certain inherent rights." In the floor debate on the Declaration, the point was made that Mason's assertion could not be applied to slaves because they owned no property; that they were, in fact, *themselves* property. As we shall see, this application of Locke's theory eliminated the most formidable legislative hurdle to the enactment of Mason's proposal. Locke provided additional help to white Virginians as they struggled with their fantasies about the nature of black humanity. His linkage of property with full citizenship was also enormously useful to the slave-owning founders, in that it provided a powerful theoretical rationale for the distinction between masters and slaves, and a rationalization for ill usage of the latter. If slaves were merely property—cogs in the production machine, like plows and horses —their harsh treatment in the interest of greater productivity could not really be deemed inhumane. This was no corruption of Locke's theories: he had been no Leveller.

Through his work, however, Locke had struggled against theories of government that justified absolute monarchy. In marshaling the idealistic strands of the political theories that had come down to him and moving them forward in order to destroy forever the notion of the divine right of kings, he had imposed on the government a moral obligation to society and to the individuals it comprised. In a hierarchical and paternalistic world where the weight and worth of human beings were always tied tightly to property—the sovereign kings of the realm, nobles with vast estates whose assertions of their own rights made the initial inroads into monarchical authority—an intellectual journey all the way to the Levellers was inconceivable. In Locke's context, the assertions of limitations on government and of immutable individual rights represented a major contribution to notions of human freedom.

Political theorists and the pamphleteers of political protest provided the intellectual culture from which the main ideas of the American Revolution would grow. But there was another nutrient that the founders absorbed with their mother's milk. It didn't have to be studied and reflected upon; it was there, writ large, in the lessons that living taught each and every day—in slavery.

Consequently, after Bacon's Rebellion of 1676, itself largely a product of anti–Native American sentiment, when it seemed politically desirable and economically necessary, it was easy and natural to firm up the already established position of blacks as perpetually bottom-dwelling, lifelong, and hereditary human chattel.

So as Virginia's founding fathers moved into the ten-year period preceding the firing of the first shots at Lexington and Concord—they had been handed a rich bouquet of ways to understand the world, including the freedoms due to Englishmen of substance, disregard and even contempt for the English lower orders, the view that Native Americans were dangerous exotics, and the "knowledge" from daily life that blacks were both irretrievably inferior and, at the same time, indispensable to them.

The point is made quite clearly in the recollections of George Mason's son John:

> It was very much the practice with Gentlemen of landed and Slave Estates . . . so to organize them as to have considerable resources within themselves. . . . Thus my father had among his slaves Coopers, Sawyers, Blacksmiths, Tanners, Curriers, Shoemakers, Spinners, Weavers & Knitters, and even a Distiller. . . . All these operations were carried on at the home house. . . .
>
> My father kept no Steward or Clark about him. He kept his own books and superintended, with the assistance of a trusty Slave or two, and occasionally with some of his Sons, all the operations at [or] about the home house. . . . In carrying on these operations to the extent required, it will be seen that a considerable force was necessary, beside the House Servants, who for such a household, a large family and entertaining a great deal of company must be numerous.

But arguably most important in terms of America's racial order was the idea that the Virginians wanted recognition as English aristocrats. They deeply resented being treated as inferiors or in-debted junior partners in international commerce. They were people who, as a class, needed all the psychic props they could find. And so their position at the top of a society shot through with inequality was enormously significant to them. Feeling slighted by their English "equals," they depended on their "bond-men and bond-women" both to enable them to live in style and to validate their social status. As the historian Nathan Huggins has noted, slaves supplied their owners with a major source of "their power as men."

The colonists wanted nothing less than to be recognized as equals by the aristocrats of England. The Byrd and Mason letters both cry out for such acknowledgment. When Mason, the slave owner, took up the notion of equality in his Declaration of Rights with no hint of irony, it was not simply because he under-stood Locke's natural laws to extend rights only to those who owned property and were therefore "members" of society; it was also because he was looking across the Atlantic, at England's king and governing aristocrats. That is to say, when Mason proclaimed human equality and freedom, he was aiming his words at those who exercised power over *him,* not dropping down a welcoming cloak in which to enfold those over whom *he* exercised power. In this he was absolutely a typical member of his class.

The amending of the Mason draft on the floor of the Virginia Convention closed the circle. Conservatives who were still trying to slow the push to independence believed that the broad sweep of the language Mason used in his assertion of equality was a weak point upon which they could capitalize. Using the dreaded image of slaves thrusting for freedom after being inflamed by the promise implicit in Mason's words, the conservatives sought to derail the Virginia independence project. Ultimately their attack was blunted by an amendment that read, ". . . and have certain in-herent rights, of which, *when they enter into a state of society,* they cannot by any compact deprive or divest their posterity." Mason biographer Robert A. Rutland reports that the colonel remained silent during this debate. Whatever ambiguities may have been in

Mason's heart, it was clear that in the general view of Virginia gentlemen of 1776, only *some* men were created equal, and whatever the turbulence of the middle 1770s had brought, it was not to be a "side wind" disturbing arrangements regarding either property or production. Considering the privileges they enjoyed and the cultural and technological boundaries within which all of these gentlemen Virginia founders lived, it was an achievement, albeit a crimped one.

CHAPTER 2

Bright Promises, Shadows of Sin

. . . it is too clear for dispute, that the enslaved African race were not intended to be included, and formed no part of the people who framed and adopted this declaration. . . .

The unhappy black race were separated from the white by indelible marks, and laws long before established, and were never thought of or spoken of except as property and when the claims of the owner or the profit of the trader were supposed to need protection.

. . . [Moreover, at the time of the Revolution, blacks were deemed to be] beings of an inferior order, and altogether unfit to associate with the white race, either in social or political relations; and so far inferior that they had no rights which the white man was bound to respect.

Dred Scott v. Sanford, Howard 393 (1857);
Roger Taney, Chief Justice, writing the majority opinion
for the Supreme Court of the United States.

Ten years elapsed between the time Mason wrote his letter to the London merchants and drafted the Virginia Declaration of Rights. The difference between the two documents owes as much to the profound political, intellectual, and emotional changes that had occurred in the eleven years between the Stamp Act crisis and the year of independence as it does to the documents' disparate purposes. The first, written from inside an evolving yet well understood and fairly stable colonial order, was a wail of complaint wrapped around an assertion of American innocence and a plea for recognition of the colonists as Englishmen of standing.

The second was a confident assertion—in the face of terrifying uncertainties about the future—of how the people of Virginia were beginning to define themselves. The political and intellectual effort that brought about these changes laid the foundation for the new American nation and did much to justify the exalted reputation of the entire founding generation—not just the four slave-owning Virginians being considered here.

Think of the marvelous political work the Virginia patriots accomplished between 1765 and 1776. Until they began to be prodded by the English government's ruthless pursuit of additional revenue, and then by Parliament's haughty insistence on its prerogatives, the American colonies were essentially separate extrusions from England. The seacoast towns—Boston, Providence, New York, Philadelphia, Baltimore, and Charleston—each had more contact with London, Liverpool, and various ports in the West Indies and Africa than they had with one another.

There were precious few bases for common trust and understanding among the colonies, and no mechanisms for achieving them. Moreover, had common undertakings been proposed prior to the Stamp Act crisis, they would have been met by the familiar restraints of inertia and loyalty to the Crown. If any such stirrings had been detected, royal governors would surely have been as quick to discourage those fraternal impulses as, say, high-end employers of our own day are to demonize salary comparisons between professional employees.

The stunning achievements of the 1765–1775 period were not only instances of resistance to specific obnoxious acts of the British government but also key stages in the development of a continental revolutionary consciousness and impulse toward self-government, as well as the creation of the rudimentary instruments to carry out those purposes. From the organization of the Stamp Act Congress to the establishment of the Committees of Correspondence and the convening of the Second Continental Congress (which was in session in Philadelphia as Mason was preparing the Virginia Declaration of Rights in Williamsburg), the Englishmen who were becoming Americans engaged in an intense and explosive ten-year orgy of democratic political activism. It is one of their most powerful but least noted legacies to us, a timeless primer for aspiring democrats on how to do the work of democracy.

All of the practices and arts of politics were deployed in that fruitful decade. The colonists paid careful attention to public affairs. They spent time alone exploring and honing their opinions on important issues by reading history and philosophy as well as the latest correspondence, dispatches, and political tracts. They thought hard about what was occurring and consulted with others in order to inform and sharpen their views. They became involved in local and colonial politics by standing for office and putting forward proposals for action. When necessary—when, for example, colonial legislatures were disbanded, or when new instruments for protest and self-governance were required—they crafted appropriate new mechanisms. But most of all they thought, talked, debated, listened to one another, wrote, and created in ever-widening circles. All the while, their activities were fraught with great personal, political, and financial risk.

Creative self-governance, even under the best of circumstances, is very hard work. Not everyone involved will be intelligent. Not everyone will be well motivated. Not everyone will be a team player or without ego (to say the least). Maturity, industriousness, patience, perseverance, determination, a clear sense of achievable ends, tolerance for human foibles, intelligence, steadfastness, and good humor are among the qualities necessary for effective participation in such enterprises. The conditions in which these men did this work were far from ideal. Colonial governors and their agents were ever watchful for treasonous activity and ready to mete out punishments whenever they could. And there were other citizens who, if not exactly agents of the Crown, were nonetheless deeply loyal to it and ready to support it in a variety of ways. Yet the patriots pushed on. The separate entities of 1765 had by the late spring and early summer of 1776 created a Continental Congress, established a Continental Army with its own commander in chief, drafted Declarations of Independence in scores of localities and a number of former colonies, agreed on a national Declaration of Independence, and put before the Congress a proposal for developing a new and permanent plan of government for the new republic. They had also sorted themselves out and brought forth from the various colonies one of the most talented collection of statesmen-politicians ever assembled to lead a nation.

Mason, Washington, and Jefferson all played their parts in these momentous events, while Madison, just twenty-four in 1775, began his apprenticeship in statecraft.

Mason's most valuable contribution throughout these days may not have been in any direct action he took but rather in his subtler role as mentor to and encourager of his younger neighbor Washington. Not only did these men share proximity and local interests; they were both also deeply interested in land and its acquisition. Mason was known to possess one of the colony's keenest legal minds in regard to real estate, and he had avidly added to the considerable landholdings his parents had left him. Washington had started out as a surveyor and learned about the vastness of the West while carrying out that work and through his army service during the French and Indian War. Having inherited a modest estate from his father, he had augmented it by inheritance from his half-brother Lawrence and then increased it enormously by marrying Martha Custis, a very rich widow. With her money he bought even more land.

Land and slaves were two of the principal preoccupations of the gentry, so the bond between these two neighbors and plantation owners was tight long before 1765. Washington had become a member of the House of Burgesses in 1759, joining Mason, who was then serving a single term in that body. Mason later declined to stand for reelection because he was disgusted by legislative log-rolling and long-windedness. Instead, he became intensely active in local Fairfax County affairs. Thus, by the time of the Stamp Act crisis, many years worth of rich and amiable discussions about land, slaves, agriculture, and colonial and local politics had already taken place between the two neighbors. Surely Washington recognized Mason's intelligence, learning, insight, and steady judgment.

Perhaps most illustrative of the Mason-Washington collaboration was an exchange that occurred in April 1769, when Washington learned of the northern colonies' plan to oppose recent acts of Parliament that would impose new taxes on imports and limits on political action in the colonies. The colonists were groping toward an association of colonial merchants who would agree to forgo any importation of nonessential English goods, thereby damaging England's economy. Washington considered the idea and then wrote to consult Mason:

> At a time when our lordly Masters in Great Britain will be satisfied with nothing less than the deprication [*sic*] of American freedom, it seems highly necessary that something should be done to avert the stroke and maintain the liberty which we had derived from our ancestors; but the manner of doing it to answer the purpose effectually is the point in question. . . . That no man should scruple, or hesitate a moment to use a[r]ms in defence of so valuable a blessing, on which all the good and evil of life depends, is clearly my opinion; yet A[r]ms, I would beg leave to add, should be the last resource, the denier [i.e., *dernier*] resort.

Mason, his mind running in the same channel as but a bit ahead of Washington's, was ready to respond. He prepared a draft that put his and Washington's impulses into concrete form. It incorporated the resolutions already developed in the northern colonies but was tailored for a plantation economy. In a provision that would later be dropped by the Virginia legislators, Mason called for withholding tobacco from export until the problems were resolved. Mason's draft also called for "plain living"—that is, the use as far as possible of goods produced in America rather than the more upscale provisions usually obtained from England. Washington took Mason's document to a meeting of the House of Burgesses in May. The House began its work, but Governor Botetourt, appointed to his position by the Crown, soon realized that the body was contemplating a strong protest against the British Parliament's new legislation. Exercising the political privilege of his appointment, Botetourt quickly dissolved the assembly.

The Virginians reconvened in the Raleigh Tavern, where Washington presented Mason's paper. The Mason-Washington proposal was adopted, and Virginia joined the boycott of imported goods. By presenting the proposal, Washington, formerly a back bencher (albeit a respected one), became one of the leaders of Virginia politics. Participating in this event was a brand-new member of the House, a tall, lean man from Albemarle County: Thomas Jefferson, then twenty-six years old.

Five years later, the British responded to the Boston Tea Party with the harsh Boston Port Act of 1774, and colonial resistance flared once more. Again Mason and Washington reacted against the Crown, and Jefferson, now deeply involved with the patriots, weighed in independently with what now appears to have been his first major step on the road to immortality.

Washington and Mason collaborated on a set of resolutions designed to give guidance to a Virginia Convention called to deal with the Port Act crisis. Although Mason, to Washington's disappointment, remained unwilling to return to the House of Burgesses, he was so disturbed by the ramifications of Parliament's harsh response to the Boston Tea Party that he prepared twenty-four resolutions spelling out the position of the colonists up and down the seaboard, outlining their rights and setting forth their grievances. The resolutions were presented to a meeting of the Fairfax freeholders by their chairman, George Washington. Mason's draft was a strong reiteration of the colonists' arguments against parliamentary overreaching, joined to a new program of nonimportation of British goods, expressing the desire that " 'an entire stop' could be put to the 'wicked cruel and unnatural' slave trade. . . . "

The "Fairfax Resolves," as they were called, contained a ringing statement of both deference and independence that left the colonists hanging delicately on the precipice of treason: "It is our greatest wish, and inclination, as well as interest, forever to continue our connection with and dependence upon the British government; but, though we are its subjects we will use every means which Heaven hath given us to prevent our becoming its slaves." Mason was forty-nine when he drafted this document.

The Resolves, including the call for the convening of a Continental Congress to deal with this urgent situation, were approved by the freeholders and taken on to Williamsburg by Washington for consideration by the Virginia Convention.

For his part, Jefferson repaired to his mountaintop and composed his own philosophical declaration of the position in which the colonists now found themselves. Entitled "A Summary View of the Rights of British America," it outlined positions more radical than those found in Mason's work or in most of the other writing coming out of the colonies. It was intended for the Virginia Convention, which Jefferson himself was unable to attend due to illness. He sent his essay in his stead. "A Summary View" was radical in that it denied *entirely* Parliament's right to legislate for the American colonies. Jefferson acknowledged the Crown's sovereignty over those colonies, but claimed for them equal status with England under royal rule. The thirty-one-year-old lawyer-legislator added a flourish that would later come to be recognized as typically "Jeffersonian": "These are our grievances, which we have thus laid before his Majesty, with that freedom of language and sentiment which becomes a free people, claiming their rights as derived from the laws of nature, and not as the gift of their chief magistrate. Let those flatter, who fear: it is not an American art. . . . Kings are the servants, not the proprietors of the people."

"A Summary View" proved to be too extreme for the Convention, which laid it aside, but Jefferson's admirers had two hundred copies printed up. It commanded respect in Williamsburg and later at the Congress in Philadelphia, and it was noted in London—with, of course, little acclaim. Jefferson had begun to establish his reputation as an elegant advocate of the patriots' cause and a serious political philosopher.

The First Continental Congress was held in the fall of 1774 in Philadelphia. Washington, now clearly one of the leading men of Virginia after his successful championing of the Fairfax proposal in Williamsburg, was alone among our four founders in attending that first Congress. There he cut a striking figure and earned great admiration from representatives of other colonies for his wealth, his dignified bearing and composure, and his military background. The Congress agreed on a new nonimportation program to begin near the end of 1774 and also resolved to convene a *second* such Congress should it become necessary. Tensions between the colonies and the British government escalated so much during the next few months that the second Congress was hastily scheduled for May 15, 1775. But before it could convene, the war of words was preempted by the shots fired at Lexington and Concord on April 19.

Even before that news of war in the colonies reached Virginia, the possibility of an uprising was a serious topic of contention among its citizens. Lord Dunmore, the royal governor of Virginia, probably reacting to the recent Virginia Convention to select and instruct delegates to the Second Continental Congress, ordered that all the gunpowder stored in a magazine in Williamsburg be removed and placed on a British naval schooner offshore. Alarmed, the colonists began organizing an armed force to resist the governor. They also sent a delegation to him to insist that the powder be returned because it might be needed to defend *against a slave uprising.* Dunmore defended his decision by saying that he had removed the powder to a safe place because of reports of just such an uprising in a neighboring county.

It is very probable that the "slave uprising" was an exercise in smoke-and-mirrors deception by both sides. As such, the exchange tells more about the place of blacks in the psyches of Virginia's whites at the start of the Revolution than it does about either side's actual need for the gunpowder. At more than 40 percent of the population, blacks were everywhere in revolutionary Virginia. There was a sharp conflict between slave owners' desire to have ambulatory property as an obedient extension of their will and the immutable fact that blacks were human beings with intellects and wills of their own. The fact that slaves often tested or defied their masters' designs and had been known to plan retaliatory violence either alone or in concert was an abiding topic of conversation among and a constant source of anxiety for the owners. The practitioner-beneficiaries of the violent enslavement of blacks were haunted by the idea of retributory black violence. As the historian Robert Middelkauff has put it, "The possibility of a slave rebellion was never far out of white consciousness, a possibility regarded with horror."

Even as the news from Massachusetts made its way south, armed Virginians were gathering in Fredericksburg. Peyton Randolph, the leader of the Virginia delegation to the Congress, advised the men who were planning to march on Williamsburg that the governor was in a tight corner and believed his honor to be at stake. Randolph implored his compatriots to disband, and they complied. Washington, poised in Mount Vernon to join the force gathering in Fredericksburg, turned his attention instead to his return to the Congress. When he arrived in Philadelphia in early May, he learned that two groups of colonials—one from Vermont, under the command of Ethan Allen, and the other from Connecticut, under Colonel Benedict Arnold—had taken Fort Ticonderoga, on Lake George. The news only intensified the sense of impending war. Massachusetts wanted the Continental Congress to raise a large army representing the unified colonies; New York wanted to know how to react to the British forces that were expected to land there. Congress petitioned the king for a redress of grievances and sought a restoration of peace, but the tension did not abate. Washington began wearing a military uniform and was appointed chair of a committee charged with developing plans to stockpile military supplies. Pondering his charge and developments in the field, he wrote, "Unhappy it is . . . to reflect that a brother's sword has been sheathed in a brother's breast and that the once happy and peaceful plains of America are either to be drenched with blood or inhabited by slaves. Sad alternative! But can a virtuous man hesitate in his choice?"

Washington surely intended no more irony here than Mason had when he wrote in the Fairfax Resolves that "we will use every means which Heaven hath given us to prevent our becoming . . . slaves." Raised to believe that humans needed to be augmented by ownership of property in order to claim the weight and heft of citizenship, neither man could conceive of anything more humiliating than that Parliament should have the power to strip colonists of their property. Taxes imposed without representation by a distant and arbitrary Parliament meant to the colonists that their property was always at risk. Without property, they would be rootless and without identities. They could then be blown about by any chance wind, sent hurtling this way and that, recognized and honored by no one. Mason and Washington, occupying the loftiest places in Virginia's social and political firmament, undoubtedly did view the condition to which they feared Parliament might reduce them as "slavery." This was no empty metaphor to these Virginia planters. They knew in their souls what real slaves were, knew the anonymity and misery of those poor souls' daily lives and the contempt in which they were held. No wonder, then, that though they expressed regret over the situation, Washington and Mason felt they had no choice but to fight.

In mid-June 1775, Congress decided to raise an army, for which they needed a commander in chief. Desiring to ensure that the organized military force would be seen as a Continental Army despite the fact that it was being formed around Boston, John Adams, perhaps the most influential member of Congress, nominated Washington, a Viriginian, for the post. Washington appeared embarrassed and diffident at the nomination, but several factors recommended him to his fellow congressmen. First there was the impressive military reputation (a reminder of which he wore on his back each day) he had won during his demonstrably valorous service in the French and Indian War. Then there were his quiet but commanding presence and his enormous wealth (he was judged by some at the time to be the richest man in the colonies). After limited debate, he was chosen to lead America's first army. He was forty-three years old.

When Washington took command of his army in Cambridge, Massachusetts, on July 3, 1775, his ranks were thin, his officers were in disarray, and his troops needed training and discipline. He brought to the job personal authority, a knack for handling details, a knowledge of how legislatures worked (which was to be a great asset to him in coping with constant congressional supervision

and inconsistent material support), stern self-discipline, and a sure
touch in dealing with soldiers and their officers. He was an excellent judge of men. He had a commanding presence, and his affil-
iation with the army would have a profound impact on both mo-
rale and order.

Much as he needed men, Washington felt there was no place
in his army for the 20 percent of Americans who were black, and
he issued an order to that effect. His old Virginia nemesis Lord
Dunmore took the opposite approach: the man who would be the
last royal governor of Virginia invited slaves to join his forces and
promised freedom to those who did so. Washington's famous temper flashed at this news, and he wrote to his friend Joseph Reed
that Dunmore was an "Arch Traitor."

Dunmore was surely no traitor to the king, as, in a strict sense,
Washington himself was. Yet the leader of an armed rebellion
against the monarchy under which he had been born was now
calling the human symbol of that monarchy in his own colony a
traitor. A traitor to what, then—to white people? Washington,
despite severe political tensions, had courted Dunmore at Williamsburg social events just a few months earlier in his never-
ending quest for the vast tracts of western lands that he thought
were due him for service rendered in the French and Indian War.
In the mind of George Washington—himself a man (by the standards of his time and peers) of unquestioned integrity and virtue—the bonds of class and whiteness should have transcended
revolutionary enmity. A few weeks later he made a more practical
response, permitting the reenlistment of free blacks who had already served at Lexington or Concord or Bunker Hill, on the
ground that otherwise they might take Dunmore up on his offer.
Although slaves were not to be enlisted under the new policy, the
historian Benjamin Quarles informs us that "manpower needs"
ultimately trumped racism, and both slaves and free blacks were
signed up for duty in the Revolution. The fighting was to grind
on for more than six long years, during which Washington's character, political acumen, and leadership skills would hold the army
(and therefore the Revolution) together and earn him immortality. During that struggle, 20 percent of the eventually victorious

army—a number equivalent to the percentage of African Americans in the colonies—would be black.

Over the next few months, colonies and localities struggled to define the new political reality that their armed hostility with the mother country had reaped. Even though they were obviously in rebellion, many colonists were tempted to shy away from the clear implications of what they had begun. Independence and democracy were frightening unknowns, and visions of unrestrained volatility, particularly among the masses of ordinary people and, of course, slaves, made many hearts faint. Finally, however, on May 10, 1776, the Congress adopted a resolution suggesting that colonies whose Crown-appointed governments were no longer functioning establish new governments such as the representatives of the people deemed suitable. John Adams, brilliant and determined leader of the congressional drive for independence, was elated, calling the resolution "the most important [step] that ever was taken in America."

Ironically, it was the Virginians, holders of more slaves than any other colonists, who moved with the greatest alacrity in response to the congressional suggestion. Mason, who had been typically crotchety about his perennial dissatisfaction with legislative work after the 1775 Virginia Convention (he had complained to Washington about the babblers, pettifoggers, and factions and expressed his doubts about whether a successful revolution could be carried out by such men), returned to Williamsburg in the spring of 1776 and was immediately put in charge of developing the new plan of government.

One of the men eager to help with this work was a youngster new to colony-level politics, James Madison, who would find in Mason a mentor and a model. Ralph Ketcham, one of Madison's biographers, describes their initial encounter this way: "A wealthy planter, often aloof from colonial politics, Mason was nevertheless widely acknowledged as having the most profound understanding of republican government of any man in Virginia. . . . He assumed immediately the leadership of the committee, and his proposals became the basis for the famous declaration of rights and plan of government subsequently adopted by the convention.

Presumably Madison did not know the stout, gouty Mason until his late appearance in Williamsburg, but from that moment on, Madison's admiration for the older man scarcely ever wavered."

Jefferson, too, desperately wanted to be a part of the process of drafting the new plan for Virginia, but he bowed to the wishes of his political leaders that he continue his service in the Continental Congress. His interest in the Virginia plan remained so great, though, that he prepared his own draft and forwarded it for consideration in Williamsburg.

That June, in Philadelphia, Richard Henry Lee submitted a proposal calling for the Congress to declare the colonies free and independent. A drafting committee composed of Benjamin Franklin of Pennsylvania, John Adams of Massachusetts, Robert Livingston of New York, Roger Sherman of Connecticut, and Thomas Jefferson of Virginia was appointed to draw up such a document. John Adams would later recall that he had prevailed upon Jefferson to prepare the first draft because he was a Virginian and wrote brilliantly. Adams thought it important that a Southerner be prominent in creating the national declaration so that independence would seem the project of the entire nation, not just that of the zealous New Englanders.

Adams's choice, though he could not have anticipated it at the time, would prove to be one of the most important in the shimmering line of lustrous contributions he was to make to his country during his lifetime. Jefferson was exactly the right man for the job. As the historian Joseph Ellis has explained,

> Throughout the remainder of his long career Jefferson never again experienced a challenge better suited to call forth his best creative energies. The work had to be done alone, isolated from the public debates. It needed to possess an elevated quality that linked American independence to grand and great forces that transcended the immediate political crisis and swept the imagination upward toward a purer and more principled world. Finally, it needed to paint the scene in bright, contrasting colors of truth and falsehood, right and wrong, 'ought' and 'is' without any of the intermediate hues or lingering doubts. It is difficult to imagine anyone in America better equipped, by disposition and experience, to perform the task as well.

Jefferson worked on the document in his boardinghouse. He later said that he did this work without consulting any book or pamphlet. Maybe. But surely he would have kept a copy of his own version of a Virginia constitution. Moreover, Mason's draft of the Virginia Declaration of Rights was published in Philadelphia just as Jefferson agreed to take on the chore.

In any event, he did his work, and after some important final polishing, first by the other members of the drafting committee and then by the Congress, the nation was offered what would become the most famous sentence in American political literature: "We hold these truths to be self-evident: that all men are created equal; that they are endowed by their creator with certain inalienable rights; that among these are life, liberty & the pursuit of happiness. . . ."

The specter of slavery looms large here. Some years earlier, the young Thomas Jefferson had attempted, in the House of Burgesses, to soften the harshness of slavery and even to clear the way for the manumission of some slaves. His initiative had been firmly rejected. Then, in the preamble to his own draft Virginia constitution, he had included a prohibition on "holding in slavery any person henceforth coming into the country." He had accused the king of pursuing his absolutist goals by, among other things, "promoting our negroes to rise in arms among us; those very negroes whom by an inhuman use of his negative he hath refused us permission to exclude by law." But just as Jefferson's earlier effort had not been incorporated into the body of Virginia laws, so the second effort did not find its way into Virginia's constitution.

In his draft of the Declaration, Jefferson leveled the following charge against the king:

> He has waged cruel war against human nature itself, violating its most sacred rights of life & liberty in the persons of a distant people, who never offended him, captivating and carrying them into slavery in another hemisphere, or to incur miserable death in their transportation thither, this piratical warfare, the opprobrium of *infidel* powers, is the warfare of the *Christian* king of Great Britain. Determined to keep open a market where MEN should be bought & sold, he has prostituted his negative for suppressing every legislative attempt to

> prohibit or restrain this execrable commerce: and this assemblage of
> horrors might want no fact of distinguished die, he is now exciting
> those very people to rise in arms among us, and to purchase that lib-
> erty of which *he* has deprived them, by murdering the people upon
> whom *he* also obtruded them; thus paying off former crimes com-
> mitted against the *liberties* of one people, with crimes which he urges
> them to commit against the *lives* of another. . . .

While this remarkable paragraph did not make it through the
editing process on the floor of the congress, it is nonetheless one
of the most intriguing pieces of prose ever to come from Jefferson's pen, in that it directs our attention not to things existing in
the world outside the author's skin, but rather toward things deep
within his soul. It is clear from these few sentences that Jefferson
had thought hard about slavery's horrors. He notes that the "distant people" had never offended the king, and he is keenly aware
of the hideous perils of the Middle Passage and of the "miserable
death" that so many suffered. He gives a deadly accurate description of slavery as a "cruel war against human nature itself." From
1769 through the mid-1780s, Jefferson made repeated legislative
efforts to alleviate slavery. But when he finished his work on the
Declaration, he was thirty-three and owned more than a hundred
men, women, and children.

Perhaps part of the answer to this conundrum can be found in
an observation by one of Jefferson's biographers, Willard Sterne
Randall. Commenting on the sudden increase in Jefferson's
wealth when he inherited more than a hundred slaves from his
father-in-law, Randall writes, "Ironically it was slavery that suddenly made Thomas Jefferson free of his tedious, unremunerative
law practice and enabled him to devote his energies to American
freedom." Viewed in that light, and given the quotidian facts of
Jefferson's life at home in Virginia, his indictment of the slave
trade—the longest and most ornately rhetorical of his charges
against the king—is truly stunning. What could have prompted
Jefferson to inflate the crisp twenty-nine-word thrust he had
composed for the Virginia constitution into the bloated roar of
rage that he chose to place so dramatically near the end of his draft

of the Declaration? The historian Pauline Maier, who has written incisively about the creation of the Declaration of Independence, suggests that the passage marked "the emotional climax of his case against the King." If so, Jefferson surely must have thought the slave trade a weighty matter, and felt that the king's veto of Virginia's legislative attempts to end the importation of slaves raised a compelling moral argument against the humanity of the sovereign.

But if the trade itself was horrible, could its purpose—slavery—be any less so? None of the manifold horrors of slavery was an abstraction to Jefferson. These were the tactile facts of his everyday life.

Those facts do not square, however, with the decent and outraged sentiments Jefferson poured into his indictment of the king. While he would attribute the Congress's decision to eliminate this charge to the insistence of Georgia and South Carolina on keeping the slave ports open, and to northerners' lust for the profits of the trade, cooler heads surely noted the wide discrepancy between Jefferson's rhetoric and the facts on the ground at places such as Monticello, Gunston Hall, and Mount Vernon. To lay all the blame at the feet of the king was to ignore the way Americans of both North and South had enriched themselves and their emerging nation by means of this "execrable commerce."

The only suggestion in Jefferson's broadside of American complicity, the concession that there was a "market where MEN can be bought and sold," is diluted by the surrounding assertions that the king was determined to keep that market open and that he had misused his veto to override the honorable efforts of the Americans to end the commerce. Moreover, Jefferson in no way acknowledges the belief of many who understood the economics of slavery that a cessation of the *international* trade would immediately make the excess slaves of the Virginians more valuable on the *domestic* market.

After all is said and done, any parent of more than one child will recognize this impulse as a deeply human reaction to trouble: blame somebody else. How many times have we parents heard the anguished cry of one sibling accusing the other, "He did it!" or, "She made me do it!"

We have heard such denials of guilt from Virginia slave owners before. Byrd, for example, with his bondmen and bondwomen, played up the innocence of American life in contrast to the fleshy pleasures available in London. Mason, too, looked out serenely from the vantage point of his "retirement" and recorded his contentment "with the blessings of a private station." When he noted of his English cousins that "we are still the same people with them, in Every Respect," and followed up with the American kicker "only [we are] not yet debauched by Wealth, Luxury, venality & Corruption," he put words to a very ugly delusion that has been perpetuated for more than two centuries since.

How can we account for the coupling of assertions of Virginia innocence with charges of English corruption? How can we explain the morphing of the slavery charge in Jefferson's draft for the Virginia Convention into the rhetorical excess with which he intended to end what was then the most important writing he had ever done? This seems to me beyond mere hypocrisy. It appears to be the product of the irreconcilable tension between earned guilt and the aspiration to honor.

In June and July 1776, Jefferson felt the added tension of having to justify his slave-owning culture while giving deference to the new nation's "decent respect to the opinions of mankind." It was a task too difficult even for his formidable mind and pen. It was as if the profound clash in his soul forced out that gusher of overheated rhetoric, that jumble of charges disconnected from reality. Among the Virginia patriots, the worm of conscience worked away beneath all effective structures of denial. And so their claims of innocence reverberated throughout the land as their last shield against an unpalatable truth. Innocence and guilt were twinned and driven deep into the core of American culture.

Jefferson's compulsion to include such a charge in the Declaration of Independence clearly undercuts Chief Justice Taney's assertion in his *Dred Scott* opinion that blacks "formed no part of the people who framed and adopted this declaration." Only in white people's imagination were blacks not a part of the *people* who created the Declaration. And those blacks were in that Congress, deep in the psyches of all the men who had floated to the top in a slave society and who had to deal on a daily basis with black human beings, as opposed to the black abstractions that would slog through Taney's mind eighty years later.

Taney's formulation that blacks "were never thought of or spoken of except as property" can be accepted only if the blacks of that day are seen as inanimate objects. Things can be defined that way, but human beings are terribly hard to pin down with mere words, particularly in a society in which words are used to redefine the truth of active existence. Lord Dunmore and General Washington proved that. Dunmore claimed to have taken the gunpowder out of Williamsburg because a slave rebellion was rumored to be in the works, and the colonists claimed to need it back because *they* had to have it to protect themselves from just such an uprising. Inanimate objects don't rebel. People do.

If the blacks who fought at Lexington and Concord and later at Bunker Hill were not part of the *people* who framed the Declaration, then of course neither were their poor white comrades in arms. But while Jefferson was drafting the Declaration and Congress was editing his work, some black soldiers were fighting under Washington, and other blacks under British command. Free-thinking if not free-willed, they chose different routes to freedom.

The fact is that without black Americans, including the 40 percent of Virginians who were black, the America that General Washington led into revolution in 1775 would have been a vastly different place—a poorer and weaker place, much less capable of waging a successful revolt. And Mason, Washington, Jefferson, and Madison might themselves have been poorer, better, less conflicted, and more honest. I would argue that they might also have been less learned, less strategically astute, and less politically wise. Blacks and their works were present in the Revolution as essential elements both of its strengths and of the Virginians' greatness.

CHAPTER 3

The Wages of Privilege

We started out with a flawed Constitution, but we fixed it.
Justice Thurgood Marshall

Prior to the Civil Rights Movement, supporting black rights was often a lonely and courageous enterprise for whites, in large measure because even in white liberal circles, black inferiority, or at least the need to improve the morals, skills, and intellect of most blacks, was a given. Syrupy calls for "toleration" were frequently heard. For blacks, who suffered mightily at the hands not only of poor, illiterate, and ignorant whites but also of highly educated and rich ones, the word *toleration* was like a lash to the soul. People tolerate fools, pests, and stray animals that their children bring home. We were none of those. We were full human beings and full Americans, and *toleration* suggested that we were something less.

Moreover, we believed that our stature was derived from "nature and nature's God," as Jefferson might have put it, and from the Constitution of the United States and the Declaration of Independence—though we had survived nearly two hundred years, since their institution, of evidence to the contrary. The idea of "toleration" infuriated us because it suggested that whites had the right to bestow status on us (and of course, if they could bestow it, they could also withdraw it).

Way back at the Virginia Convention in the early summer of 1776, the young James Madison spotted in one of Mason's rights proposals the line "all men shou'd enjoy the fullest Toleration in the Exercise of Religion, according to the Dictates of Conscience. . . . " After a bit of parliamentary maneuvering, the sentence was reworked according to Madison's design, to read, "all men are equally entitled to the free exercise of religion, according to the dictates of conscience. . . . " The clear-eyed Madison had eliminated the implication that there was some supervising secular power that had the right to bestow, and therefore to rescind, the full right to religious freedom. For him, the idea of "toleration" as the basis for the rights of citizenship was anathema.

In late 1777, when he was just twenty-six, Madison was elected to serve in Virginia's Council of State under Governor Patrick Henry. He would remain on the council until the end of 1779, by which time Thomas Jefferson had succeeded Henry. It was during this period that an intimate, enduring friendship developed between Madison and Jefferson. In December 1779, Madison was appointed to the Congress. Delayed by a hard winter, Madison, accompanied by his slave Billey, finally made his way to Philadelphia to take his seat in March 1780. He was then in a perfect position to see the trouble that a weak central government foretold for the new country, and to observe how little the Articles of Confederation, ratified in March 1781, would do to rectify the situation.

At this time the war was going badly for the patriots, and Congress began to defer increasingly to the states instead of exercising the national sovereignty that the emergency demanded. Madison arrived in Philadelphia just in time to see Congress relinquish to the colonies the authority to issue currency. Washington described the moment as a point when the authority of the new nation was leaking from its principal source to thirteen different seats. As inflation raged throughout the colonies and the successes of the British campaign in Georgia and South Carolina mounted, he watched members of the Congress, enmeshed in their local concerns, dither ineffectually.

By the time Madison left the Congress at the end of 1783, he was convinced that if the country was to survive, the national government must be more "energetic" than it was permitted to be under the Articles of Confederation. He had seen state delegations raise local interests above national needs on such disparate issues as monetary policy, the contention over whether Vermont would be admitted into the union, the claims of existing states to western lands, and the difficulty of obtaining adequate provisions for Washington's ragged and struggling army. He observed interstate disputes, such as one between Maryland and Virginia concerning the Potomac River, as stunting the possibilities of national economic growth. Once out of the Congress, he watched as the weak and bedraggled new nation, situated as it was on the potential for boundless wealth in the future, was stalked by the predatory giants of Europe—Great Britain, France, and Spain. And he saw the nation become even more debilitated as currency issued by the states fueled inflation, encouraged speculation, and sparked sharp money practices that discouraged the productive hard work and saving habits that would really build the economy.

Hoping to develop a better way for the nation to cohere and grow, Madison decided to undertake an intensive program of study and research on republican government. He asked his friend Jefferson, now the American minister in France, to scour the bookstalls of Paris for all the scholarly treatises he could find dealing with the history and practices of republican government. His request resulted in a "literary cargo" of treatises on political thought and history that was delivered to Montpelier in the winter of 1785–86.

Madison devoted the first six months of 1786 to research and reflection on the nature and forms of government. The title of a paper he wrote at the time, "Of Ancient and Modern Confederacies," gives a sense of the scope of his investigations. At the end of his intense scholarly endeavors, Madison recorded "the facts and lessons about the ancient and modern confederacies in a booklet of forty-one pocket-sized pages, easy to use in debate or writing."

In August 1786, he left Montpelier for Annapolis, where he was to attend a meeting commissioned by the Congress to "examine the trade of the states . . . and consider . . . a uniform system in their commercial regulations." No quorum was assembled because it was clear that a number of earnest delegates, including Madison and Alexander Hamilton, were intent on using the meeting to strengthen the federal government. There were many strong interests in the nation that were profiting handsomely under the weak national government and wanted to scuttle the Annapolis gathering; they did so by not attending, and thereby precluding a quorum. Those who did attend issued a call for a convention to be held in Philadelphia the following May, to consider the problems of the union.

The opposition had several components. Besides the profiteers, there were entrepreneurs pursuing grandiose schemes involving foreign countries, who understood that a government with more strength at the center would hinder their activities. Some simply feared the unknown, while others distrusted republicanism because they worried that it would disintegrate into "mobocracy." Still others felt that a strong central government with a strong executive smelled too much like the monarchy that had just been thrown off, with such difficulty and at such great cost.

By 1786 Madison was no longer a fledgling politician waging a novice's campaign. He was a formidable figure. And this little powerhouse and his fellow nationalists were as determined to prevent the development of a home-grown form of monarchy as they were to halt the disintegration of the country because of a weak national government. In 1787 Jefferson noted that Madison had

> acquired a habit of self-possession, which placed at ready command the rich resources of his luminous and discriminating mind, and of his extensive information, and rendered him the first of every assembly afterwards, of which he became a member. Never wandering from his subject into vain declamation, but pursuing it closely, in language pure, classical and copious, soothing always the feelings of his adversaries by civilities and softness of expression, he rose to the eminent station which he held in the great National Convention.

In order to bring together a harmonious and powerful Virginia delegation that could lead the way at Philadelphia, Madison had to satisfy both George Washington and Governor Edmund Randolph. Randolph was a jealous champion of states' power, while Washington understood the urgent need for an authoritative central government to rule the emerging nation. Madison supposed that if he could weave a cloth that could bind these two concerns, he might have a plan that could succeed in Philadelphia. So from his seat in the Congress, now meeting in New York, Madison corresponded with both men and devised a plan of "mixed government," in which the constituents of the national government were states, not individuals. The central government was charged with preserving national dignity, local self-government, and the freedom of the people.

Madison's letters became the basis of the Virginia plan—the outline that would ultimately be laid before the convention in Philadelphia as the foundation of the debates about the new Constitution.

George Washington was asked to join a seven-member delegation to Philadelphia; appointed by the Virginia Assembly, it counted among its members George Mason. Deeply distressed by the selfish and shortsighted behavior of the states, Washington was also alarmed by reports of a rebellion in Massachusetts and concerned about the threat it posed to the new nation. Daniel Shays and his followers—described as "desperate and unprincipled men" by Secretary of War Henry Knox—sought to extract an economic-justice principle from the Revolution, including an abrogation of all debt. In pursuing this aim, they forced a closing of the courts in Concord. Although the rebellion ultimately fizzled, the episode pointed to a weakness in American governance that the British had merrily predicted and thoughtful Americans had begun to fear. Notwithstanding his concern, Washington, even after being prodded by Madison (whom by now he firmly respected), was reluctant to reenter politics.

His first response to the invitation to be a member of Virginia's delegation was a soft no. Washington had pressing debts and was very short of ready cash; his brother had just died, and his favorite niece, Fanny, had just lost a baby; and he worried that if he became a member of the Convention, he would be breaking the promise he had made to the nation, when he sheathed his sword in 1783, that he would henceforth forswear public service. Then, too, it was possible that the states would treat the Philadelphia convention as cavalierly as they had the previous one, in Annapolis; if so, it would mean a loss of face. Washington seemed to be calibrating what effect his decision to go or not go would have on the enormous renown he had earned during the Revolution. On the one hand, he worried that his reputation might suffer if he attended and the convention failed; on the other, he knew he might lose respect if he didn't demonstrate sufficient support for republican principles. Ultimately, Madison's subtle and deft wooing and the urgings of Washington's other friends, coupled with his own deep concern that the new nation was still far too fragile for its own good, led the general to agree.

However haltingly his decision came, the news that the hero would attend surely precluded a repeat of the disastrous Annapolis experience. Most states mustered rosters of their most distinguished men for service in Philadelphia. Both Benjamin Franklin and George Mason expressed their admiration for the quality of the delegates, with Mason avowing, "America has certainly, upon this occasion, drawn forth her first characters."

When Washington arrived in Philadelphia on May 14, he received a hero's welcome: he was escorted into town by the Philadelphia Light Horse and saluted by bells and cannon. Madison was already there and working hard to firm up the Virginia plan. In order to facilitate this process, Madison had arranged for the entire Virginia delegation to stay together in the same rooming house, but Washington decided to accept grander accommodations at the home of financier Robert Morris. Mason was present at the Indian Queen Tavern for the preliminaries, but he reverted to his normal cantankerous self during the lull before the actual convention began. Early on he declared that he was "heartily tired of the etiquette and nonsense so fashionable in this city."

Nevertheless, by the time the seven delegations required for the convention to do its work assembled on May 25, the Virginians, spurred by Madison and with Mason's participation, had already put the finishing touches on their plan. In addition to Madison, Washington, and Mason, the Virginia delegation consisted of Governor Edmund Randolph (the delegation's chairman), the lawyers John Blair and George Wythe, and a physician, Dr. James McLurg. On that first day, Pennsylvania nominated Washington to serve as president of the convention. The motion was seconded by South Carolina, which expressed the hope that the motion would pass unopposed. It did. Washington assumed the chair with due modesty, and the work of revising the government of the United States began in earnest. Although he presided conscientiously, Washington took no significant part in the debates, joining in only once, and that at the end. He certainly did not contribute to the floor debates that shaped the Constitution. Nevertheless, the very presence of the most revered man in America, and his obvious determination to see the project through to a successful conclusion, provided much of the glue that kept a long, arduous, and contentious process moving through a long, uncomfortable summer. Moreover, his participation surely lent the proceedings great credibility throughout the country and sharply enhanced the prospects of ratification.

Washington made another immeasurable contribution to the outcome of the summer of 1787 through his constant socializing when the sessions were in recess. His biographer James Thomas Flexner puts it this way:

> History will never be able to assess the extent of the contribution Washington made through such personal contacts, but it was surely great. His years of military service and his hospitality at Mount Vernon had made many of the delegates already his friends or acquaintances; his personal prestige was awesome even with those who had not previously met him; and he had, to a superlative degree, the gift of finding beneath controversy common ground.

Madison's role, meanwhile, was so active as to make him appear almost superhuman. Not only did he intend to promote and defend the plan of which he was the principal author; he also assumed the onerous burden of becoming the official scribe of the convention. His studies had convinced him of the importance of keeping a good record of all proceedings that created confederacies. Thus he said of the duty,

[I] chose a seat in front of the president member, with the other members on my right and left hand. In this favorable position for hearing all that passed, I noted in terms legible and in abbreviations and marks intelligible to myself what was read from the Chair or spoken by the members; and losing not a moment unnecessarily between the adjournment and reassembling of the Convention I was enabled to write out my daily notes during the session or within a few finishing days after its close in the extent and form preserved in my own hand on my files.

The great struggle between the large and small states represented the most serious threat to the whole enterprise. The Virginians, particularly Madison and Mason, were committed to the idea of popular representation in the new national legislature. The small states, fearing the power of the larger ones and suspicious of their land claims in the West (especially the Virginians', including Mason and Washington), and leery of the sentiments of the general public, argued for equal representation.

Mason's passion for constitutions of the "democratic kind," on display a decade earlier at the Virginia Convention, was powerfully carried onto the floor in Philadelphia. He acknowledged the basis for the fears of those who opposed popular elections, but insisted that no government was free of "imperfections and evils." He argued for the rights of the people and asserted that the representatives "should think as [the people] think, and feel as they feel."

A large part of the opposition to popular elections was the sour view that many of the delegates had of the essential nature of the common man. One of the main arguments against a republic for the United States was that history taught that such forms of government often led to tyranny by single-minded majorities. Another was that republics were subject to anarchy. Bolstering these arguments were the recent examples of Shays' rebellion and the corrupt legislature of Rhode Island. When Mason's belief in the rights of man proved insufficient to overcome these qualms, Madison supplied stronger medicine.

Madison maintained that an extended republic, based on consent and endowed with a strong central government, was the best remedy for human weakness. He understood and accepted the moral frailty of human beings and the possibility that republican forms of government might lead to instability. In his view, however, an extended republic comprising many contending voices would serve as a balance wheel. It would provide outlets for argument and at the same time tamp down the disruptive effects of any one line of contentiousness as it struggled to find its place in the whole range of voices in the democratic chorus. Madison's argument prevailed, and it was agreed that the new House of Representatives would be based on popular representation.

Before they reached that point, though, the delegates had to decide precisely what "popular representation" meant. Would slaves be included, or would they not? Under the Articles of Confederation, each slave had been counted as three fifths of a person. Now, at the Constitutional Convention, South Carolina attempted to bloat southern representation by suggesting that slaves be counted equally with whites, on the ground that a slave's labor produced as much wealth as the labor of a white worker.

The position embraced by the South Carolinians and their allies was nakedly cynical and exposed the contradictions inherent in the holding of human beings as property. Slaves, though themselves powerless, had always equaled power. The slave owners used their slaves to improve their lives and augment their status, and this newest argument was directly in line with that de facto policy. Political interests and swollen egos allowed such men to believe that *they* could raise the status of blacks when it suited their purposes. In effect, while operating an utterly inhumane scheme of production, they now demanded a representational bonus for the evil they were doing. As for the slaves themselves, the inevitable result of their being counted one-for-one with whites would have been to deepen substantially their pit of misery.

Predictably, the North ferociously resisted the idea of one-to-one representation, arguing that it would be warranted only if the blacks were granted citizenship. Compromise became possible only when the Southerners retreated to the ratio that had been contained in the Articles of Confederation: each slave would be counted as three fifths of a person. But even three fifths of a loaf would prove sufficient to give the South undue influence in national affairs up until the Civil War. The compromise that was deemed necessary to preserve the nation also preserved for posterity a mathematical expression of the cruelty and inhumanity at the core of American culture.

The debate on this subject put George Mason in a most difficult position. In principle, he was powerfully opposed to both slavery and the international slave trade, but he was also a Southerner and a slaveholder. On this occasion, his principles carried his vote: he vowed that he would quit the convention before he would agree to let slaves be counted, which he felt was equivalent to including tacit approval of slavery in the Constitution. But when the vote was taken and went against him, Mason did not leave. Instead, in an unsuccessful attempt to relieve the founders and the Constitution of the immortal odiousness of the decision to weave slavery into the basic legal and political fabric of the nation, Madison would introduce a semantic fix, substituting the prim word *persons* for the unambiguous *slaves*.

The issue of slavery could not be so easily put to rest, however. It arose again in a fierce dispute over the regulation of international trade. Since slavery was itself the result of the most hateful form of international commerce, it was poetic irony that such an argument should occur at the Constitutional Convention, a principal purpose of which was to ensure that the new nation would be able to do business effectively, both from state to state and with the rest of the world. Southerners, believing that northern shipping and industrial interests would construct the rules of trade in ways that would benefit them at the expense of the South, pressed for a requirement that a two-thirds supermajority pass all measures regulating trade. The North resisted, infuriating George Mason, who was doubly distressed to learn that Northern interests were willing to join with Georgia and South Carolina, states that were less concerned about the imposition of burdensome trade regulations than they were about the preservation of slavery.

Luther Martin of Maryland, in proposing either an outright prohibition on the importation of slaves or a tax on such importation, neatly summed up the dilemma by damning the slave trade as inconsistent with the revolutionary theories of freedom based on natural law.

John Rutledge, a former governor of South Carolina, responded heatedly to all such ideas, insisting, "Religion and humanity have nothing to do with this question. Interest alone is the governing principle with nations. The true question at present is whether the Southern states shall or shall not be parties to the Union. If the Northern states consult their interest, they will not oppose the increase of slaves which will increase the commodities of which they will become the carriers."

This brought an explosive retort from Mason:

> The present question concerns not the importing states alone but the whole Union. . . . Slavery discourages arts and manufactures. The poor despise labor when performed by slaves. They prevent the immigration of whites, who really enrich and strengthen a country. They produce the most pernicious effect on manners. Every master of slaves is born a petty tyrant. They bring the judgment of heaven on a country. As nations can not be rewarded or punished in the next world they must in this. By an inevitable chain of causes and effects, providence punishes national sins, by national calamities.

The spirit of the Revolution had inspired the new Americans, so that by the 1780s every state except Georgia had enacted legislation barring the slave trade. Yet when the issue emerged from committee, the Northerners had defeated the supermajority proposal and paid off their debt on the international-trade issue by supporting their Southern allies. Constitutional protection for what Mason had branded the "infernal trade" was conferred for a period of twenty-one years.

Madison shared Mason's moral distaste for the slave trade, but his driving passion was always to create a stronger government. That led him to accept this compromise that enhanced and protected slavery. By the time the slave-trade issue flared, he had seen the delegates overcome a series of disputes that might have torn the convention apart. He could envision a strong, rich nation growing out of this work, and the alliance between the New Englanders and South Carolina and Georgia posed a significant threat to his cherished goals. So Madison acceded to their position and again settled for a solution that merely kept the ugly word out of the document. The evil was hidden behind this tidy facade in Article I, Section 9, of the Constitution: "The Migration or Importation of such Persons as any of the States now existing shall think proper to admit, shall not be prohibited by the Congress prior to the Year one thousand eight hundred and eight, but a Tax or duty may be imposed on such Importation, not exceeding ten dollars for each person."

Having tasted the fruit of corruption, the members of the convention later added an affirmative protection for slavery: "No Person held to Service or Labour in one State, under the Laws thereof, escaping into another, shall in Consequence of any Law or Regulation therein, be discharged from such Service or Labour, but shall be delivered up on Claim of the Party to whom such Service or Labour may be due."

In a superficial sense, Mason and Madison had succeeded: the words *slave* and *slavery* did not sully the nation's basic charter. The founding fathers had their fig leaf of decency. But the underlying reason for their reticence—their *shame*—endured. Their political genius had failed to address the enormous horror of the massive theft of life, hope, and labor that had provided a substantial part of the wealth, bravery, and brainpower that made their freedom possible. Instead of extending liberty to the slaves, the Constitutional Conventioneers intensified their anguish.

As August turned into September, most of the delegates began wanting to be done with the work and to return home. However, George Mason and a trio of like-minded delegates felt that a number of matters had not yet been given sufficient attention. Mason was concerned that the executive power would be too great and the brakes on that power—including impeachment and the process for amending the Constitution—too weak. He worried

about corruption at the top of the government and about the possibility of a backslide toward monarchy. And finally, he was intent
on preserving the rights of citizens. In his final argument, Mason
once again complained that the inability of the new government
to prohibit the international slave trade for twenty-one years
would weaken the country.

Many of Mason's objections might have been overcome if the
convention had addressed a proposal put forth by Mason and El-
bridge Gerry of Connecticut, calling for the addition of a bill of
rights to the Constitution. The many opposing delegates, however (including Madison), responded with an argument buttressed
by the theory of natural law. Governments had only such powers
as were given to them by the governed, they argued; the government being created in Philadelphia was a government of enumer-
ated powers, which did not include the power to invade the rights
of citizens. They also pointed out that the individual states had
their own bills of rights and that therefore the federal document
needed no such protection.

When Mason lost on this major point, he resolved not to sign
the document. Despite some attempts to use language to paper
over differences, and an eloquent plea from Benjamin Franklin for
unanimity, Mason wouldn't budge. He did not sign the Constitution, and he shared his misgivings with some Philadelphians.
Those views, soon published and given wide circulation, were the
seedlings from which Anti-Federalist objections to the Constitution would grow. Mason left for home in the company of James
McHenry of Maryland, "in an exceeding ill humour indeed," as
observed by Madison.

Both Madison and Mason took up leadership roles for their respective positions. An enduring and shimmering part of Madison's legacy is his authorship, along with Alexander Hamilton and
John Jay, of "The Federalist Papers," a powerful set of arguments
for the ratification of the Constitution, which were circulated
during the period when the state conventions were considering
such ratification. Mason, for his part, helped lead the Virginia opposition along with Patrick Henry and Richard Henry Lee.
While Madison and the other Federalists were able to thwart Ma-

son's and the other Virginians' plans to force a second Constitutional Convention to consider amendments, the opposition *was* strong enough, finally, to force Madison to promise that amendments would be offered during the sitting of the First Congress. Taken together, those amendments would become the Bill of Rights.

Although there were surely base motives in play on each side of the debates about ratification, there were also serious and principled arguments as to the best course for the new nation to take. The Federalist position flowed from a recognition of the weaknesses inherent in the attempt to govern the country under the Articles of Confederation. Such weaknesses, it was feared, would stifle almost all good intentions and invite foreign contempt and, worse, foreign meddling.

Nonetheless, many Americans, having just rebelled against a central authority that had endeavored to impose controls on liberty, were leery of giving up enormous power to a *new* central authority. Mason and his followers wanted at least some written safeguards for the freedoms they felt were essential to American liberty. Small farmers and frontiersmen, fearful of a rule by plutocrats, sought a government that rested on a broader democratic base than they believed the Constitution provided. They were concerned about such elitist filtering provisions in the Constitution as the creation of the Electoral College and the election of senators by state legislatures. They believed that the surest way to bind people to the new nation was greater and more direct participation in decision-making by the people. Despite Madison's dim view of them, it can hardly be argued that those who honestly sought either stronger guarantees of freedom or a broader-based democracy, or both, were simply "selfish, parochial, ignorant or unscrupulous." There were doubtless some in that camp who were all of those things, but there were many others who were just as honorably worried about the future of the nation as Madison.

Although the Federalists won the battle, the much-debated amendments were presented and ultimately ratified in December 1791. These were, in some substantial form, derived from Mason's Virginia Declaration of Rights. If Madison had been the "father of the Constitution," then Mason was surely the "father of the Bill of Rights," epitomizing in his argument and conviction the soul of the opposition. But Mason's achievement occurred late in his life, and his last efforts elicited the ugly charges that the great mind was dimming. Contradictory testimony offered by dispassionate observers—Jefferson among them—indicated that this was no more than slanderous fulminating by his Federalist political enemies. Still, Mason paid an even higher price than diminished reputation. Friendships that had once been warm and nourishing were now cold and hollow, including his near-lifelong relationship with George Washington.

Mason was to die in October 1792, less than a year after the Bill of Rights was added to the Constitution. One is left to wonder whether he would have been comforted during his last days had he known of the actions of Peter Sublett of Powhatan County, Virginia, in 1788. Inspired by the powerful freedom force Mason had helped set loose in the American spirit, Sublett, a minor member of the landed gentry and a stong supporter of the Revolution, wrote a letter that opened with these words: "I believe *that all men are by nature equally free & independent* and therefore from a clear conviction of the injustice and criminality of depriving my Fellow Creatures of their natural and dearest Right, do and heareby emancipate or set free the following Men, Women, and Children"(*ital.* added). Ultimately, fifteen people were freed by this document.

Mason had what we would now call a strong libertarian streak, powerful common sense coupled with an independent spirit. He stood a bit outside the culture into which he was born, and was thus able to raise issues about it that continue to reverberate in our national life today.

Even after the Constitution and the federal government were in place, there remained a brooding question about whether or not the new country could hold together. Prominent among the new self-created Americans were the members of the Virginia plantation class, who, as we have seen, had been raised with an English hierarchical cast of mind. They were certain that the people best fit to run the country were among their number. They had such a great personal stake in the country and its commerce that they were convinced their class would be able to discern the national interest and, as men of affairs, bring the best judgments to bear on major national issues. That was how they had run Virginia, and it is surely how they must have viewed the matter of running the country.

In *Cultural Life of the American Colonies,* Lewis B. Wright describes the situation in Virginia this way: "There was a huge gap between large planters and small freeholders—a chasm that grew wider as the eighteenth century wore on. Most economic and political power was in the hands of great landowners. Small farmers sometimes grumbled but often accepted the situation silently— and sometimes stirred themselves to overt hostility."

Members of the planter class enjoyed the good life that their social elevation required. Their great houses on the banks of rivers, filled with fine furnishings from Europe, and their entertainments boasting elaborately laid tables all attested to this. Many of these men went into considerable debt with English firms in order to maintain themselves in this manner. In *Patriarch: George Washington and the New American Nation,* Richard Norton Smith gives us a glimpse of how the culture transmitted by Washington's older half-brother Lawrence fit on the shoulders of the future president:

> The youthful Washington emulated Lawrence's stylishness, refusing on one occasion to venture into the woods without nine shirts, six linen waistcoats, seven caps, six collars, and four neckcloths. He longed to be part of the fashionable society that swirled around the older man's Potomac estate, named for the British admiral Edward Vernon. After Lawrence's marriage in 1743 to Anne Fairfax, whose father served as agent for his cousin Lord Thomas Fairfax, the proprietor of 5 million acres in Virginia's Northern Neck, young George could study at first hand the graces of Tidewater Virginia. He excelled on the dance floor, relished card games, and was not above attending cockfights.

However superior the Virginians may have felt themselves to be, though, their alarm over the weakness and inefficiency of the government under the Articles of Confederation cannot be dismissed as mere self-dealing. Government by Congress alone was insufficient for the national purpose, especially when the powerful pull of individual state sentiment was added to the mix. (Even so great a contributor to the founding as Thomas Jefferson, for example, meant Virginia, not America, when he referred to "my country.") Moreover, predatory hostile nations such as Spain, England, and France were forever skulking around the frontiers of the new nation, probing at weak spots and itching to pick at the carcass should the fledgling state stumble and fall. Finally, there were dangerous centrifugal forces within the confederation itself, as men of great ambition saw power, wealth, and fame that might be had by pulling this or that part of the new nation away and aligning it with other interests.

Madison made a massive contribution to the stability of the new nation through the Constitution. He must first be recognized for his political acumen in discerning the need for a new political dispensation, and for his skillful efforts over the years in bringing the convention into being. Having applied his extraordinary intellect to the study of all possible constitutional forms, he put together a carefully reasoned working draft that gave the convention a good basis for its work. Then he lobbied wholeheartedly during and after the convention to create the document and get it ratified.

Madison at thirty-seven was a fully mature political man who had already made an indelible mark on American history by virtue of his distinct set of personal characteristics. He had a prodigious intellect and was strongly motivated to make the new nation work. He was a hard worker whose most constructive instinct was always to burrow through the most difficult political and theoretical problems until he found a solution. He did not possess the charisma to accomplish his goals through the grand gesture, nor the tongue or pen to win his ends by elegant turns of phrase. James Madison was, in modern parlance, a "grind." But he was a grind whose patience with other men's foibles, egos, and bluster made it possible for him to be a formidable presence in the legislative chamber. He was a tiny human being with an enormous will that harnessed a cluster of extraordinary talents in the service of the new nation.

George Mason's devotion to freedom, and to the creation of a charter of rights to ensure that freedom, was matched only by his devotion to his family, his plantation, and his local community. His mind and spirit contributed the basic American charter of rights, and then his crotchetiness and his independence—which surely caused his old friends and colleagues great grief and cost him dear friendships—succeeded in helping to force the Bill of Rights into the Constitution. Legal brilliance, a mature independence, and a fierce commitment to liberty were the ingredients that made possible Mason's great final contribution to his nation.

And even Jefferson, away in Paris serving as minister to France during this period, played his part, sending Madison the books on politics that enabled him to do his original research and, in the end, make the suggestion about adding amendments during the first session of Congress, *after* ratification, which provided the solution to the Virginia political problem.

Mason's political role ended with the ratification of the Bill of Rights, but during his last days, he was at peace with the new government and pleased by the deference and respect that Jefferson, at least—who had been away during the heat of the ratification fight—continued to pay him. Mason's contributions to the new nation were far less visible than those made by the others, who were more willing to leave Virginia and to work on the national stage (one of Mason's final political acts was to turn down an opportunity to represent Virginia in the Senate during the First Congress). Yet in mentoring his fellow Virginians' revolutionary thought and fierceness of spirit, he gave an enormous gift to the nation. While Jefferson and Madison surely learned from Mason, it was his close neighbor Washington who was the principal beneficiary of his wisdom. Washington's rise to prominence in Virginia politics—a necessary prelude to his rise in national politics—was based in some large degree on the fruits of his relationship with his older, more intellectual friend. Mason was, in the end, a superb tutor in the arts of government and revolutionary politics.

Washington believed that the development of a new and much stronger government for the nation had averted a looming national crisis. He had relied on younger men, particularly Madison and Harry Lee, through the ratification process, and he may have felt that with the potential crisis deflected—in part because of his own huge contribution of prestige and gravitas—he was entitled to go home to Mount Vernon for good. Now fifty-five years old, he had led a rugged life and was acutely in need of cash. He possessed vast holdings of land and slaves, but his income was diminished because he had been unable to supervise his farms during the Revolution and had decided to stop selling slaves.

One has to wonder, however, whether Washington could actually have entertained any realistic expectation that he could avoid being called to the presidency—and whether, indeed, he really *wanted* to avoid it. After all, he was by now used to being the first man in America, and to all the adulation and deference that went with that status. Could he really imagine sharing that space in his lifetime and in the history books with someone else? If so, he was a different man from the one whose concern for his reputation had initially made him reluctant to go to Philadelphia.

In any event, through early 1788 the newspapers were full of Washington-for-president sentiment. Letters from friends and old comrades in arms poured in to Mount Vernon, reminding him that there was no possible alternative to his becoming president. One such letter came from a source close to his heart: according to Douglas Southall Freeman, the French general Lafayette, who had been Washington's dearest ally, wrote to express "some alarm over the magnitude of executive powers under the Constitution but voiced the belief that if Washington exercised the authority and found it dangerously great he would reduce it. For this and other reasons, Washington must consent to be President."

That was the nub of the problem. People didn't know what a president was—how much power he should have, or how he should act. They knew only about being governed by kings, and there were those who still believed that without the centripetal force of a monarchy to hold it together, any society was doomed to fly apart. Yet many were also afraid that the new Constitution might allow a man with lordly aspirations to turn the office into a semimonarchy. Nevertheless, a president couldn't be just an ordinary street fellow; he had to have enough grandeur to help bind the nation together and make it proud. The people were full of uncertainties, but there was one thing they were sure of: they had Washington, and he would know what to do. It was Washington's stature that had given the citizenry some comfort about the creation of the presidency in the first place.

The attributes that commended Washington so highly to his colleagues and contemporaries were embedded in real events that all concerned remembered personally. Washington's achievements as commander in chief were complemented by his character, as evidenced by his leadership qualities and his voluntary relinquishment of power at the end of the war. When Washington had first assumed command of the army, at Cambridge in 1775, Abigail Adams had reported to her husband, "You had prepared me to entertain a favorable opinion of General Washington, but I thought the half was not told to me. Dignity with ease and complacency, the gentleman and soldier, look agreeably blended in him. Modesty marks every line and feature of his face."

By 1787, Washington had acquired vast holdings and worldwide fame. He internalized all of his success and status into a personality that was already marked by iron discipline and a certain coolness. In addition, he was imbued with such values of the old Romans as self-possession and civic honor. Marcus Cunliffe, an insightful observer of the American presidency, believes that the general had a strong sense of gravitas (and its uses) and practicality: Washington, he writes, "linked past and future . . . by occupying himself doggedly with the present [and] being magnificently matter-of-fact."

The people of the United States showed their support by turning the Independence Day celebration of July 4, 1788, into a national Washington-for-president rally. Washington finally let the election happen; he was the unanimous choice of the presidential electors. In April 1789, after all the ballots had been tallied and certified by Congress, Charles Thomson, the designated congressional official, arrived at Washington's doorstep at Mount Vernon and read the general a prepared statement, which said, in part:

The proofs you have given of your patriotism and of your readiness to sacrifice domestic separation and private enjoyments to preserve the liberty and promote the happiness of your country did not permit the two Houses to harbour a doubt of your undertaking this great, this important office to which you are called not only by the unanimous vote of the electors, but by the voice of America.

Washington, for his part, had a response ready. He read from a paper he had prepared:

Sir, I have been long accustomed to entertain so great a respect for the opinion of my fellow-citizens, that the knowledge of their unanimous suffrages having been given in my favor, scarcely leaves me the alternative for an option. Whatever may have been my private feelings and sentiments, I believe I cannot give a greater evidence of my sensibility for the honor they have done me, than by accepting the appointment.

I am so much affected by this fresh proof of my country's esteem and confidence that silence can best explain my gratitude.

What was Washington being asked to accomplish? First, to hold the country together. Second, to take care of the nation. And third, to define the presidency itself. And he would go on to do these things in just the way he had led the revolutionary army to success: with the help of the best brains he could enlist, he would plug away at whatever problems his days brought him, persistently, with common sense, and with an impressive sense of honor nuanced by reserve and personal rectitude.

He was convinced from his own observations and from the tutoring he had received from Federalists such as James Madison that the government of the United States needed to be substantially stronger and more "energetic" than was permitted under the Articles of Confederation. Embedding the Constitution and the government it created into the flow of life in the new nation was Washington's last great challenge. He summarized his approach as he and the Senate worked to develop protocols for their interchanges: ". . . as the Constitution of the United States, and the laws made under it, must mark the line of my official conduct,"

Washington said, "I could not justify my taking a single step in any matter, which appeared to require their agency, without its being first obtained." This "energetic" government had to be achieved according to the rules, and the president, just like any other citizen, had to respect those rules and properly defer to the other branches of government. But Washington was also surely determined that the government so conducted would be "energetic" enough to stabilize the new country and enable it to grow.

That set of goals, more than anything, explains his siding with Treasury Secretary Alexander Hamilton in the struggles over the latter's financial plans for the United States, including the assumption of revolutionary debts, the floating of a foreign loan, and the chartering of a national bank.

Much has been made of the clashes of politics and personality between Hamilton and Secretary of State Thomas Jefferson, as their pivotal disagreements grew personal and then led to the formation of the first American political parties. Washington's method of leadership undoubtedly had a great deal to do with this titanic clash. The president understood his own limitations and knew the value of advice offered by good minds. So he leaned hard on these two very different men, his principal advisers.

Hamilton was a driving city man, up from nowhere and on the make, a man of finance who appreciated the power of markets and money in the evolving definitions of men and states. A member of the original circle of Federalists, he, like Madison and others, had been alarmed through the early and mid-1780s by the siphoning off of federal power by the states, as each seized the authority to issue its own currency. Jefferson, by contrast, was a rather dreamy and self-indulgent rural aristocrat, an idealist who hoped that the new nation would provide better conditions for human development than the churning urban commercial life he had seen in Europe, which he considered hopelessly corrupt. For all their differences, the two men were similarly ambitious—the Northerner thrusting and direct, the Southerner indirect and often devious in pursuing his goals.

After hearing his two secretaries out on their dispute over the financial plan for the country, Washington backed Hamilton because his approach seemed to offer the surest route to a strong centralized government and national unity. Believing that controlled passion was required in practicing democratic government, Washington was at first perplexed and then quite troubled by the intensity of the personal animosity that developed between the two cabinet officers. His concern prompted him to try to bring about a reconciliation between the men, an attempt at mediation that took the form of a letter that the president wrote to Jefferson in the late summer of 1793, ostensibly regarding the urgent possibility of an Indian war:

> How unfortunate, and how much is it to be regretted . . . that whilst we are encompassed on all sides with avowed enemies and insidious friends, that internal dissensions should be harrowing and tearing our vitals. . . . I believe it will be difficult if not impracticable, to manage the reins of government or to keep the parts of it together. . . . In my opinion, the fairest prospect of happiness and prosperity that ever was presented to man will be lost, perhaps forever. . . . My earnest wish and my fondest hope . . . is that instead of wounding suspicions and irritable charges, there may be liberal allowances, mutual forbearances and temporizing yieldings on *all sides.* Under the exercise of these, matters will go on smoothly and, if possible, more prosperously.

Washington sent substantially the same letter to Hamilton.

All of the prime impulses of the Washington presidency are on display in his letter to Jefferson. There is the devotion to unity, along with the belief in disciplined moderation in the service of democracy. There is the vision always fixed on the far horizon, no matter how vexing today's difficulties may be. And finally there is the passion for America, the surprising passion in this man who comes down to us through the centuries as a granite monument.

The ability to keep his mind focused on the overall goal and to devise tactics designed to reach that goal was a hallmark of Washington's character from at least 1775 to the end of his life. And one of the things he understood best was that by taking himself to be smaller than the ultimate goal, he could use himself as an important tactical instrument in struggling toward that goal. For example, he was well aware that he was the most powerful symbol of unity that the nation had. Thus, during congressional recesses in the second and third years of his presidency, he made an effort to travel around and show himself to the nation instead of spending the entire break at his beloved Mount Vernon.

His first such trip, in 1789, took him through the northern portion of the nation. The second, in 1791, took him through the South. Travel was arduous, and he was nearing sixty (the sixty of the late eighteenth century was a far older sixty than that of the late twentieth, and Washington had also used himself hard throughout his lifetime); probably he needed a rest. In the early 1960s, I saw Prime Minister Nehru of India, then old and so frail that he needed the constant physical support of his attentive daughter, Indira Gandhi, make a similar tour in the back of an open jeep through the state of Uttar Pradesh. I did not know of Washington's trips then, but I thought Nehru's effort constituted an act of heroic patriotism. Likewise, Washington clearly saw a need to encourage his people, then still in the process of transforming themselves into citizens of the United States.

The profound anomaly that slavery represented in Washington's makeup was teased to the surface during his unity trips. On his northern tour, Washington skipped Rhode Island because it had not yet ratified the Constitution. In August 1790, after that ratification had finally occurred, he traveled to the state to welcome it into the union and to bury old wounds. While he was there, he spoke to a Jewish congregation in Newport and delivered one of the most remarkable statements about human decency ever uttered by an American president. He said:

> It is no more that tolerance is spoken of, as if it was by the indulgence of one class of people, that another enjoyed the exercise of their inherent natural rights. For happily the government of the United States, which gives to bigotry no sanction, to persecution no assistance, requires only that they who live under its protection should demean themselves as good citizens, in giving it on all occasions their effectual support.

Do we detect the sure touch of Madison as speechwriter here?

Less than six months later, at the outset of his Southern tour, we see a very different side of Washington. The president had been warned of the potential problem posed by a Pennsylvania law under which slaves were to be freed six months after their owner had both moved into the state and become a citizen thereof. The law did not apply to the president, who remained a citizen of Virginia, though he resided in Pennsylvania. Nevertheless, Washington, who sometimes referred to slaves as "that species of property," reacted viscerally, as a propertied man. He worried that his slaves' exposure to the laws of Pennsylvania might give them an idea above their station: freedom! In order to avoid both that occurrence and any negative judgments that might be made about his own motives, the president planned a subterfuge whereby his two most valuable slaves in Philadelphia (and anyone who inquired about them) would be misled into believing that they were to be returned to Virginia for the convenience of Mrs. Washington.

How can these two actions, emanating from the spirit of a single human being and coming just a few months apart, be reconciled? Washington was not psychotic, nor did he have a tendency to lie either to himself or to others. The great sensitivity he displayed in rejecting the notion of *tolerating* one group of citizens— calling it demeaning to the "tolerated" and to the ethos of the nation—is far clearer than the insights of many twentieth-century political figures. And yet he could also fret over the possible "insolence" of blacks, and dream up devious schemes to trick them back into the firm shackles of Mount Vernon slavery.

Whatever his slaves' humanity might elicit from him in developing his slave-management policies at Mount Vernon, when he looked at them, the president saw first property and then human beings. However useful they might have been in prosecuting the Revolutionary War, however indispensable in creating his wealth and providing him with comfort, blacks existed outside the ambit of democratic decency. Slaves were lesser beings against whom bigotry could be sanctioned, persecution assisted, and deviousness employed in the service of preserving wealth and continuing subordination.

There was a real unity to Washington. Despite his passion for his new republic, he was a disciplined member of the landed gentry. The aristocrat could be haughty and distant and overly fond of pomp. He could also be worshipful of wealth and jealous of his property—including his human property. And throughout his high-minded service to his country, the old planter could still yearn for the pleasures of home—his "fig and vine," as he often said.

All of these parts of the Washington whole came together to make 1792 a troubling year for the president. He struggled, as he had throughout his presidency and as he would continue to do through his second term, with Britain, France, Spain, and the other European nations that sniffed at the ragged edges of his new country, and with the Native Americans who inhabited many of those edges and were inexorably becoming the ragged edge of the American conscience. Having contended manfully with these problems as he filled in the outlines of the presidency and helped erect the structures of the other branches of government, Washington now wanted to go home. The factionalism within the country—personified by Hamilton and Jefferson—taxed him, as did the occasional criticism of his haughtiness, which some believed hinted at monarchical aspirations. He was particularly vexed by the work of Philip Freneau, editor of the *National Gazette,* a Republican paper allied with (and often fronting for) Jefferson's views.

He had every reason to believe that he had done his part for his country and that he deserved a few quiet years of honored retirement at the end of his life. So he turned to his old aide Madison and asked for his help in developing a valedictory. But Madison and Jefferson both urged him to stay on.

Jefferson wrote, "Your being at the helm, will be more than an answer to every argument which can be used to alarm and lead the people in any quarter into violence or secession. . . . North and South will hang together if they have you to hang on."

Washington listened to the two younger Virginians and many others who offered similar views. Reluctantly, he set his valedictory aside and said nothing more about going home. His silence was taken as a willingness to serve another term, and he was unanimously elected president for a second time.

Washington's second term was far more difficult than his first. Repercussions of the French Revolution resounded: Europe drifted into war, and the strains reverberated in America. The unrestrained revolutionary government of France demanded that America repay it for French assistance in the American Revolution with military support. Great Britain, arrogantly ignoring American protestations of neutrality, interdicted American shipping and impressed American seamen. Spain, allied with France and claiming colonies across a strip just south of what was then the southern border of the United States, encouraged Indian unrest. The many pressures faced by the new country led to increasing criticism of the president. Shortly after his reelection, Washington was reviled as an aspiring monarchist by the Republican *National Gazette,* and later depicted as the doddering head of the Federalist Anglophile party. Thin-skinned and ever-sensitive about his reputation, he hated the fact that his immunity from personal attack had elapsed. He was made even more morose by the ongoing hostilities between Hamilton and Jefferson.

Trouble would continue to plague the president during his second term, as his brilliant aides dropped almost all restraint in their personal bitterness and then retired to private life as the European war and its dangers to the fragile new nation persisted. Jefferson's motives here, as elsewhere, are unclear, but there was surely a mixture of the personal and the professional at work. He was personally and professionally offended by Hamilton, and convinced that Washington preferred the Treasury secretary to him. He was also profoundly distressed that Hamilton's financial plan had been accepted as national policy, and infuriated at what he saw as his meddling in diplomacy. On the personal side, by indulging his expensive tastes and hobbies, Jefferson had dug himself into a chasm of debt. Like Washington, he loved his home, but unlike him, he coddled himself. Having urged the president to forgo the pleasures of Mount Vernon, Jefferson asserted (contrary to President Washington's opinion) that he himself could easily be replaced. Thus he sent a note to Washington in which he explained, "I . . . have no motive to consult but my own inclination, which is bent irresistibly on the tranquil enjoyment of my family, my farm and my books." He acted on this "inclination" a few months into Washington's second term.

Washington soldiered on, seeking peace with England through a controversial treaty negotiated by John Jay. While the great object, peace, was secured, British naval power ensured that British arrogance would also be served by the treaty. British ports were to remain closed to the Americans, but the British were to be permitted to pursue contraband into American ports. The British would additionally retain their monopoly on the fur trade north of the border, even as they participated in that trade within the United States. And to the dismay of Southerners, the treaty mentioned neither the return of any slaves who had been carried off nor the payment of compensation for them. The hard balance Jay had to strike between America's weakness and her great need for peace was all but lost in the furious debates stirred by French partisans in America, who were also, in the main, Washington's detractors. They viewed his emissary Jay as a coward, or worse. Richard Norton Smith, one of the chroniclers of Washington's presidency, describes the problem Washington and Jay faced this way:

> Those who knew Jay best knew better. The chief justice was a patriot, but also a realist. Had he resorted to threats or even dropped hints that the former colonies contemplated joining an armed league of neutrals in opposition to British raiders on the high seas, the men across the bargaining table would have laughed in his face before handing him his passport. In the end, Lord Grenville settled with the upstart republic on what many in Parliament, if not Congress, viewed as unnecessarily generous terms, not because he feared America's might but because he valued America's neutrality in the much larger contest with Jacobin France.

Washington's actions in this difficult situation—undertaking the diplomatic initiative, choosing Jay for the job, and then supporting the controversial treaty that resulted—provided an easy

target for his enemies, who took them as evidence of his preference for monarchy and all things British.

The French, for their part, made a different kind of trouble for
the president. After the execution of King Louis XVI, in Febru-
ary 1793, the revolutionary government sent impudent and im-
prudent emissaries to the United States to play on Americans'
strong sympathies, in an attempt to undermine the American administration's policy of neutrality. The first of these ambassadors,
Edmond Charles Genet (who presented himself as Citizen Genet), contemplated going over the president's head to appeal directly to the republican sympathies of the American people. He
commissioned American vessels to be used as privateers against
the British and worked diligently to stir up broad anti-British
sentiment.

The anguish of Washington's second term was perhaps most
clearly on display during a meeting held in August 1793, when
Hamilton and Jefferson were still in the government. During a debate about what to do about the outrageous French representative
Genet, Secretary of War Knox brandished the latest edition of
Freneau's paper, with its headline "The Funeral Dirge of George
Washington." Whether depleted by a searing and bitter exchange
that had just taken place between Hamilton and Jefferson, or just
hypersensitive about his reputation, Washington exploded. He
railed against abusive journalists and raged furiously at the suggestion that he was motivated by a need for self-aggrandizement. The
work of the day ended as the president slumped in his chair, spent
by his eruption.

But the next day he was back at work, continuing to plug away.
He felt he must respond vigorously to a rebellion of small whiskey
distillers in western Pennsylvania, seeing the unrest as a severe
threat to the unity of the nation and the legitimacy of its government. He personally led the military force that reestablished the
primacy of U.S. law, and in doing so made clear his preference for
civilian rather than military law enforcement. But his determination to preserve the unity of the nation came before all else. His
desire to keep the nation at peace and to preserve its neutrality
would be manifest throughout his second term.

After the defection of his two most brilliant aides, Washington drifted more and more into the Federalist camp. The end of his second term reflected all these things, as well as the old warrior's advancing age.

In the end, the luster of all the major players was dimmed during this period, no matter how great their overall contributions to the new nation. Thus a strongly negative view of Hamilton, undoubtedly shared by thousands of his American enemies, appears in the report of one of the shameless French emissaries: "Such, Citizen, is the evident consequence of the system of finances conceived by Mr. Hamilton. He has made of a whole nation a stock-jobbing, speculating, selfish people. Riches alone here fix consideration . . . they are universally sought after." However massive a role he had played in strengthening the national government, Hamilton's memory would always be plagued by the suggestion that his interest lay as much in the welfare of the moneyed class of New York as in the fate of the nation. There would ever after be a whiff of corruption about his name.

Jefferson, meanwhile, having sloughed off the weight of forging a new government, continued his behind-the-scenes partisanship and is thought to have contributed significantly to the president's difficulties in obtaining the ratification of the Jay treaty. Ultimately, his enmity toward the president upon whom he had urged four more years of unwanted national service would be unsheathed. Commenting in a letter to James Monroe on a report that cast Washington in an unflattering light, Jefferson almost gloated: "[The document] bears hard on the Executive . . . and though it clears him . . . of the charge of bribery, it does not give . . . high ideas of his wisdom or steadiness."

Nevertheless, over time, Hamilton would be remembered for his brilliance as an advocate for the Constitution and for his role in helping to stabilize and solidify the new nation. Jefferson would eventually rise to become an enduring national icon—a multifaceted American genius who appeared to dabble in statesmanship, reluctantly and with his left hand, while his mind was actually engaged in loftier matters of truth, beauty, and farming.

And Washington would be revived to stand as the first pillar of the nation. He was tired after two terms, and he was sometimes quite cranky. Very close to the end of his time in office, one of his slaves, Oney Judge, took her freedom and made her way north. Washington, as ever in hot pursuit of his property, wrote to the secretary of the Treasury to request that he look into a report that the young woman was in New Hampshire. At the close of his letter, Washington attempted to place the matter in context: "I am sorry to give you, or any one else trouble on such a trifling occasion, but the ingratitude of the girl, who was brought up and treated more like a child than a Servant (and Mrs. Washington's desire to recover her) ought not to escape with impunity if it can be avoided."

The Treasury secretary referred the matter to Joseph Whipple, collector of customs at Portsmouth. Whipple found the young woman and had an interview with her in which she said she would return to serve the Washingtons during their lifetimes only if she was assured of being granted her freedom at their deaths. On learning this, Mr. Nice Guy disappeared, and Washington, exercised not only at Oney Judge's "insolence" but at Whipple's lack of sensitivity to the master's position, replied angrily:

> I regret that the attempt you made to restore the Girl (Oney Judge as she called herself while with us, and who without the least provocation absconded from her Mistress) should have been attended with so little Success. To enter into such a compromise with *her*, as she suggested to *you* is totally inadmissible, for reasons that must strike at first view: for however well disposed I might be to a gradual abolition, or even to an entire emancipation of that description of People (if the latter was in itself practicable at this moment) it would neither be politic or just to reward *unfaithfulness* with a premature preference; and thereby discontent before hand the minds of all her fellow-servants who by their steady attachments are far more deserving of favor.

In this little explosion, the president gave a glimpse of insight into the nature of plantation paternalism. By this time, late in his life, he had surely moved into the category of "good" slave master. He had stopped selling slaves because he thought the practice was cruel, even though this new policy made his farms unprofitable and caused him to pile up debt. He believed in treating slaves decently. A little over a year earlier, remarking the death of a young slave, he had confided: "I hope every necessary care and attention was afforded him. I expect little of this from (Overseer) McKoy, or indeed from most of his class, for they seem to consider a Negro much in the same light as they do the brute beasts on the farms, and often treat them as inhumanely."

Washington's class consciousness is showing here, of course, as is his fundamental decency. But in return for treating his slaves well, he expected gratitude and model behavior from them. Decent treatment was a boon to be bestowed by the master, and one that could be withdrawn by him as well. Ingratitude and loss of property were occasions for righteous anger. The prerogatives of the aristocrat—including condescension toward lesser whites —were his and his alone until he decided to give them up. Woe be unto those, such as the hapless Whipple and of course Oney Judge, who dared withhold appropriate obeisance or otherwise encroach on those prerogatives.

Late in 1796, Whipple would report to Washington that Oney Judge was staying with a free Negro and that she had become engaged to a "mulatto." The last known word of Ms. Judge comes from the town records of Garland, New Hampshire, reporting her marriage there, to a Mr. John Harris, on January 7, 1797.

In his public life, the personal attacks on Washington increased in a bitter crescendo as his second term wound down. His intellect, his wisdom, and even his honesty were questioned in hostile editorials. Just before he turned sixty-four, the *Philadelphia Aurora* observed that previous celebrations of Washington's birthday "had been so extravagant that it was little wonder the President behaved 'with the insolence of an Emperor of Rome.'" As his energy diminished and the quality of his advisers eroded, the president's steadiness and common sense seemed occasionally to desert him. Nevertheless, as a matter of constitutional principle and a cornerstone in his policy of preserving peace, the president steadfastly defended his controversial treaty with Britain against furious assault by the Republicans in the House of Representatives and at Monticello.

Finally, as the summer of 1796 dragged on and the Fourth

Congress ground toward recess, Washington turned back to his plans for retirement. He sent the draft farewell statement that Madison had prepared four years earlier up to Hamilton in New York for final editing and polishing. It was published in the *American Daily Advertiser* on September 19, 1796, the same day President Washington left Philadelphia for his last presidential vacation at home.

The farewell is pure Washington (if you accept that latter-day "pure" Washington included dollops of both Madison and Hamilton, each of whom understood the mind of the old hero very well), but it is also eloquent in its ultimate revelation of the hopes of the founders for the new nation and the principles that guided Washington for the twenty-two years from the spring of 1775, when he accepted command of the Revolutionary Army, to March 1797, when the presidency was transferred from his hands into those of John Adams.

Washington wished, for his fellow citizens,

> that your Union and brotherly affection may be perpetual; that the free Constitution, which is the work of your hands, may be sacredly maintained; that its administration in every department may be stamped with wisdom and virtue; that, in fine, the happiness of the people of these States, under the auspices of liberty, may be made complete. . . .

For the sake of democratic posterity, he urged the nation to

> promote, then, as an object of primary importance, institutions for the general diffusion of knowledge. In proportion as the structure of a government gives force to public opinion, it is essential that public opinion should be enlightened.

To promote peace and neutrality, he said, Americans must

> observe good faith and justice towards all nations. Cultivate peace and harmony with all. . . . Against the insidious wiles of foreign influence (I conjure you to believe me, fellow citizens), the jealousy of a free people ought to be *constantly* awake.

Asserting that he had done his best to follow just and decent principles in his service to the nation, he admitted to human frailty and to the possibility of "many errors" committed unintentionally. And then he addressed a final word to the fellow citizens whom he would soon be joining in private life:

> . . . I anticipate with pleasing expectations that retreat, in which I promise myself to realize without allowing the sweet enjoyment of partaking in the midst of my fellow citizens, the benign influence of good laws under a free Government, the ever favorite object of my heart and the happy reward . . . of our mutual cares, labors and dangers.

In the third American presidential election, John Adams was chosen president and Thomas Jefferson vice president. After many farewell tributes, salutes, and parties honoring President Washington, the first transfer of American presidential power from one human being to another occurred on March 4, 1797. Adams described it this way: "A solemn scene it was indeed, and it was made affecting to me by the presence of the General [Washington], whose countenance was as serene and unclouded as the day. He seemed to me to enjoy a triumph over me. Methought I heard him say, 'Ay! I am fairly out and you fairly in! See which of us will be happiest.'"

Washington returned home to the honored retirement he had long craved—a planter, beloved father of his country, and famous citizen of the world. While attending to his farming and training a watchful eye on the city that he now acknowledged as the "City of Washington," the general also kept up with world affairs through correspondence and the steady flow of visitors to Mount Vernon. As the year 1800 approached, many Federalists became alarmed at the prospect of Jefferson's winning the presidency, and they began talking of reeling the old general back into the fray. When he received a letter from an old friend suggesting that he run for a third term, Washington put concrete around the two-term precedent he had already established: "Although I have abundant cause to be thankful for the good health with which I am blessed, yet I am not insensible to my declination in other respects. It would be criminal therefore in me, although it should be the wish of my countrymen, and I could be elected, to accept an office under this conviction."

A few months later, having put the final touches on his will—in which he provided for the emancipation of his slaves after his death—and having put all other things in as much order as it is possible for humans to do, the general became ill after a long December day's ride in the wet and cold. It may be that in his letter to Joseph Whipple, a little more than three years earlier, in which he'd snapped at the notion of rewarding Oney Judge's *"unfaithfulness"* with a "premature preference," Washington had unconsciously been signaling his intention to effect a posthumous emancipation.

Over the course of a brief illness during which he declined steadily, Washington bore up well under great discomfort, considerable pain, and the strong intuition that the end was near. At one point during his long day of dying, he noticed that his personal servant had been standing at the foot of his bed for hours. He motioned for the slave to sit. Later he gave final instructions to his secretary, Tobias Lear, about his burial. When he had ascertained that Lear understood his wishes, the general spoke his last words: "'Tis well." Late in the evening of December 14, 1799, George Washington died at the age of sixty-seven. The nineteenth century was fast approaching. The beginning of America was over.

CHAPTER 4

Is a Nigger a Human Being?

. . . Soon after [their return from Paris, my mother] gave birth to a
child, of whom Thomas Jefferson was the father. It lived but a short
time. She gave birth to four others, and Jefferson was the father of
all of them. Their names were Beverly, Harriet, Madison (myself)
and Eston—three sons and one daughter. We all became free agreeably to the treaty entered into by our parents before we were born.
We all married and have raised families.

Madison Hemings

In 1946, 327 years after the first twenty blacks sold in North
America were landed at Jamestown, Clay Hopper, an American
white man working temporarily in Canada, received an order
from his employer that dismayed and confounded him. Hopper
was the manager of the Montreal Royals, the top minor-league
farm team of the Brooklyn Dodgers. Branch Rickey, the general
manager of the Dodgers, informed Hopper that a black player,
Jack Roosevelt Robinson, had been signed to a minor-league
contract by the Dodger organization and was to be assigned to
Montreal to work and develop under Hopper's supervision. Robinson would be the first acknowledged black to be allowed to
work in "organized baseball" in the twentieth century. Hopper,
sharing a moral deformity that had afflicted hundreds of millions
of white Americans over the centuries, resisted the innovation
with all his might.

"Do you really think a nigger's a human being?" he asked
Rickey.

To Hopper's credit, his spirit was large enough to be affected by experience, and over time he would become one of the biggest boosters of Robinson's heroic, pioneering burst into elite American baseball. But Hopper's question about the nature and extent of black humanity was a deeply American one, formulated decades before the founding of the republic and discussed with greater or lesser nuance over the centuries since. The question was being debated in economic, judicial, political, and theological circles even as Virginia blacks were demoted in status from the level of the lowest whites to that of slaves in the middle of the seventeenth century.

A version of the same question plagued the delegates at the 1776 Virginia Convention, at which the Commonwealth's first postcolonial government was established. George Mason's draft of the Virginia Declaration of Rights was amended to exclude blacks from the assertion that "all men are by nature equally free and independent" and therefore possessed of inalienable rights. The amendment made it clear that the Virginians had concluded that the equality guaranteed by natural law did not adhere to all men who were born and breathed, but only to those who "had entered into a state of society." If the Virginia Declaration of Rights had been a Christmas gift, the amendments would have been a label reading: Blacks Not Included.

At the Second Continental Congress, the clear meaning that the Virginia Convention had attached to the idea that "all men are created equal" may have been incorporated by inference into the Declaration of Independence, since there was no recurrence of the slavery debate. The understanding implicit in the two documents was made *ex*plicit eleven years later by the delegates to the Constitutional Convention, as they pondered matters considered weightier than the human qualities of blacks: the voting power and property rights of the slaveholding South, and a favorable trade regime for the international shippers of the North.

In trying to answer these questions, whites of the day did what they always did when dealing with the status and definition of black people: they consulted one another (a practice that remains all too prevalent today). It was the most comfortable tactic for eminent white American jurists as they looked back on the involvement of blacks in the creation of the republic.

Anyone who had been paying attention, however, would have realized that blacks, living in quite awful circumstances, had been giving their own answers to the question of their human identity from the very beginning. A powerful and irresistible answer was offered in Philadelphia in the spring of 1787, when two black Americans, Richard Allen and Absalom Jones, both former slaves (whom we will return to later), collaborated to found the Free African Society, "from a love of people of their complexion whom they beheld with sorrow." Theirs is generally regarded as the first formally organized institution run *by* blacks, *for* blacks, in North America.

The evolution of black community organization from the twenty people purchased by the Jamestown colony in 1619 to the Free African Society, an entity based on love, self-respect, and charity, is a complex story. It is a profoundly human story of blacks and whites making a new country together, and a story of *both* blacks and whites reduced by slavery to something substantially less than their full human potential.

The saga of the African slave was one of fierce and dogged assertion of humanity in the face of conscienceless capitalism, pride, and fear. The horror began with some Africans' being gathered up and delivered to white slave traders by other Africans. It continued in the dungeons of the great castle warehouses on Africa's western coast, where the captives were stored until appropriate lots could be assembled for shipment. When the time came to sail, those who had not already perished or been executed for some offense were extruded naked, one by one, through a very narrow "door of no return" so they would be as helpless as possible when they were taken upon the horrendous, stinking prison vessels that would transport them to their sentences of lifelong toil under the lash—provided, that is, they managed to survive the voyage.

Olaudah Equiano, abducted from his homeland in the eighteenth century, described the experience of Africans transformed into slaves at journey's end:

At last we came in sight of the island of Barbadoes, at which the whites on board gave a great shout, and made many signs of joy to us. We did not know what to think of this, but as the vessel drew nearer we plainly saw the harbour, and other ships of different kinds and sizes; and we soon anchored amongst them off Bridge Town. Many merchants and planters now came on board, though it was in the evening. They put us in separate parcels, and examined us attentively. They also made us jump, and pointed to the land, signifying we were to go there. We thought by this we should be beaten by these ugly men, as they appeared to us; and when soon after we were all out down under the deck again, there was much dread and trembling among us, and nothing but bitter cries to be heard all the night from these apprehensions, insomuch that at last the white people got some old slaves from the land to pacify us. They told us we were not to be eaten, but to work, and were soon to go on land where we should see many of our country people. This report eased us much; and, sure enough, soon after we landed, there came to us Africans of all languages.

We were conducted immediately to the merchant's yard, where we were all pent up together like so many sheep in a fold, without regard to sex or age. . . .

We were not so many days in the merchants' custody before we were sold after the usual manner, which is this:—On a signal given, such as the beat of a drum, the buyers rush at once into the yard where the slaves are confined, and make choice of that parcel they like best. The noise and clamour with which this is attended, and the eagerness visible in the countenances of the buyers, serve not a little to increase the apprehensions of the terrified Africans, who may well be supposed to consider them the ministers of that destruction to which they think themselves devoted. In this manner, without scruple, are relations and friends separated, most of them never to see each other again.

Disoriented and frightened, the slaves were now "seasoned" by their new "masters." The American question of whether "a nigger is really a human being" probably began here. Imagine, for example, an owner such as Robert "King" Carter of Carter's Grove on the James River in the second or third decade of the eighteenth century, contemplating a fresh shipment of Africans in need of "seasoning." We know that one of Carter's methods of seasoning was minor dismemberment—perhaps a finger or a toe—of those who offended the plantation order. But might he not also have carried in his soul some of the sensibility that Jefferson tried to express, an awareness that the people whom he was about to injure and exploit had never offended him, and that his practices constituted "a war against human nature itself"? If even a whiff of such a notion troubled him, how comforting it would have been for Carter, and for powerful men like him all up and down the seaboard who were profiting in one way or another from the slave trade, to conclude that these people were not human beings at all, or that if they were, they clearly constituted a fatally degraded version of the species that would somehow be improved by being made into a commodity. Carter and his ilk could thus continue to fill their pockets and puff up their psyches as the great masters of lands and men. They could be, as William Byrd II put it, like "the patriarchs of old."

For the blacks—bewildered, uprooted, and terrified, facing lifelong imprisonment at hard labor and the contempt of their white fellow beings—there was the enormous human task of finding spiritual and human space inside one of mankind's ugliest inventions. Under such circumstances, if the human spirit does not quit and destroy itself, it is forced to seek ways to survive.

This black striving took many forms. There were two extremes. The first was abject surrender, whereby the slave clothed her or his spirits entirely in the will of the master. The essential task here was to get a close and sustained reading of the soul of the master, to anticipate in minute detail whatever desires he might have, and to satisfy them in the most ingratiating way. Ultimately the slave would hope to create living space by ensnaring the master in a web of reciprocal obligations flowing from the swell of paternalistic grandiosity.

The other extreme was outright rebellion. But rebelliousness ran headlong into one of the fundamental problems blacks have always faced on this continent: overwhelming white power and the willingness of some whites to wield it with merciless brutality. From the seventeenth century on, blacks made numberless attempts to free themselves. Virginia court records dating from the middle of that century indicate that some slaves fled imprisonment and sought freedom in the wilderness. Since blacks were held in hereditary lifetime slavery and therefore could not be punished when recaptured by having time added to their period of servitude (as could white indentured servants), owners had to come up with other methods of punishment. One involved the use of a fiery iron to brand the offender's face with the letter *R,* for *runaway.*

The word *runaway* in this context suggests an interesting cast of mind. Slaves had committed no offense against their masters and were not prisoners of war. They were simply men, women, and children who had been in the wrong place at the wrong time, and for that they and their descendants were to be horribly wronged for as long as their masters and *their* descendants could manage to continue their crimes. The slaves' bondage rested on their lack of power and on their color. In any deeply moral sense, the overwhelming fact of their lives was that their freedom had been stolen from them. That their owners had paid money for them did not change the moral reality: one cannot have a valid title to what one cannot own. Runaways had the agency not to only survive but to seek to reverse their evil predicament.

Although many individuals did risk all for a new chance at life, it was extremely difficult for most blacks to organize effectively to resist the powerful assault on them. The pervasive and brutal power of slave traders and owners systematically fractured black slave groups. Then, too, Africans in America were never a homogeneous group. The slave-gathering networks in Africa were thrown over vast areas and captured people from many different cultures, who spoke many different languages. Upon their arrival in North America, these clusters of peoples would grate against a completely separate group of blacks who had been born in this country and knew the system (and who presumably must have felt some superiority over, if not disdain for, the newcomers). There was thus no shortage of frictions for masters to exploit in the seventeenth and early eighteenth centuries.

But if the cohesion required even to imagine mounting a viable rebellion did not develop until the end of the founding period, there was nonetheless evidence of a strong black impulse to freedom many decades before the colonists launched their own revolution. Perhaps worried by Bacon's Rebellion of 1676, in which a few dispossessed black men participated, colonial officials expressed concern that some owners were permitting their slaves to gather off the plantation for funerals and other purposes; such gatherings were thenceforth suppressed for fear that they were breeding grounds for rebellion.

No one knows how many plots shaped by whispering in the night evaporated when the next sun fell on masters and their various tools of oppression. One that grew beyond whispers, however, occurred in St. Paul's Parish, Maryland, in 1739, just before Jefferson was born and when Washington was still a child. A black named Jack Ransom was said to have plotted for months, only to have word of it reach the ears of an Annapolis lawyer. The story that was boomed out across the land had two hundred blacks poised to kill the white men, marry their widows, and assert control over vast areas of Maryland. The alarm was apparently exaggerated far beyond provable fact, however, because four blacks were acquitted, and only Ransom was convicted and executed. But the damage was done: edgy whites all over the region clamped down hard on blacks' subsequent efforts to establish any semblance of an unsupervised social life. That same year, there was an actual slave uprising in Stono, South Carolina. A total of sixty-five people died before the tranquillity resulting from force could be reimposed. Undoubtedly reports of the episode traveled far and wide on both sides of the Potomac and added rich fuel to the culture of racism and paranoia in which the future owners of slaves were being raised.

Plots and betrayals were not the norm, because most of life was lived between extremes, as it is now. The way most human beings cope is to get up in the morning and make it all the way to bedtime, learning a bit more about life along the way. One thing most field slaves learned was that there was little hope of change for the vast majority of them. Hard work from dawn to dusk under a broiling sun earned them nothing except more days of hard work under a broiling sun. Still, subtle resistance might buy them a bit more time and space, so malingering, sabotage, and playing stupid were all worth a try—moderate forms of resistance, falling far short of mounting a rebellion or taking off in search of freedom.

And in some places, blacks could discern a class hierarchy. As the planters' views of themselves grew grander, so did their houses, and with that came a need for house servants whose manners and dress would help sustain the inflated notions the planters had of their own stations in life. At George Mason's home, Gunston Hall, for example, there is a painting showing James, Mason's most trusted slave, wearing Mason family livery: a knee-length, gold-trimmed frock coat with red knickers and white stockings. The contrast between this and the coarse and scanty clothing prescribed in most places for field hands could not be starker. It would hardly be human for a person such as James, given his proximity to his owner, his great responsibility, and his fine clothing, not to conclude that he was better than an ordinary field hand. Hard work, attention to detail, and, of course, acute sensitivity to the demands and needs of the master family often did earn such trusted slaves favored status and better lives.

House slave/field slave dichotomies are far too complex for exhaustive consideration here, especially since many house slaves were intimately connected to the master, either through a sexual relationship or as the offspring produced by such a liaison. In general, house-slave status did give a slave the opportunity to create some human space for himself or herself, though it also brought far closer supervision by the master family than was possible in the case of the field slave. Some slaves would use the proximity to curry favor relentlessly, even going to such lengths as to act as informers for the master. Others reversed the direction of the flow of loyalty and became intelligence agents for their fellow slaves. Many masters, fearing the growing knowledge of their slaves, would spell out words in front of them in order to preserve their secrets.

While the following, related in *The Negro in Virginia,* compiled by workers from the Writers' Program of the Work Projects Administration in the State of Virginia, took place in the nineteenth century, the story itself is common enough, and incidents like the one recounted here surely occurred in the eighteenth century as well. Susan Broaddus of Massaponax, eighty-nine years old in the late 1930s, explained to the writers that she

> was servin' gal fo' Missus. Used to have to stan' behin' her at de table an' reach her de salt an' syrup an' anything else she called fo'. Ole Marsa would spell out real fas' anything he don't want me to know 'bout. One day Marsa was fit to be tied, he was in setch a bad mood. Was ravin' 'bout de crops, an' taxes, an' de triflin' niggers he got to feed. "Gonna sell 'em, I swear fo' Christ, I gonna sell 'em" he says. Den ole Missus ask which ones he gonna sell an' tell him quick to spell it. Den he spell out G-A-B-E, and R-U-F-U-S. Course I stood dere without battin' an eye, an' makin' believe I didn't even hear him, but I was packin' dem letters up in my haid all de time. An' soon's I finished dishes I rushed down to my father an' say 'em to him jus' like Marsa say 'em. Father say quiet-like: "Gabe and Rufus," an' tol' me to go on back to de house an' say I ain't been out. De next day Gabe and Rufus was gone—dey had run away. Marsa nearly died, got to cussin' an' ravin' so he took sick. Missus went to town an' tol' de sheriff, but dey never could fin' dose two slaves.

Not all slaves' efforts to dig out a little more freedom for themselves or their fellows were so successful. While Susan Broaddus used her tongue to help Gabe and Rufus escape, Olaudah Equiano tells a story about another slave whose mouth got her into trouble. During a brief period of enslavement in Virginia, Equiano was put to work in a household where he encountered a female slave whom he described incredulously: "I was very much affrighted at some things I saw, and the more so, as I had seen a black woman slave as I came through the house, who was cooking the dinner, and the poor creature was cruelly loaded with various kinds of iron machines; she had one particularly on her head, which locked her mouth so fast that she could scarcely speak, and could not eat or drink. I was much astonished and shocked at this contrivance, which I afterwards learned was called the iron muzzle."

There were other, less exotic punishments for insubordination and sabotage, of course. There were killings and floggings and brandings and sales "down the river" away from friends and family. The masters' minds and conversations were filled with complaints about their slaves. It was inevitable: they had invested a great deal of money in this property, and it was their earnest desire that the slaves perform exactly as they willed them to and be as productive as highly paid artisans. In contrast, the slave was driven simply by the wish to avoid the lash and to find some peace. Because the masters could hope to achieve their ends only through violence, to which they frequently resorted, they feared retaliatory violence from their slaves. They were, in fact, obsessed with the possibility. They therefore endlessly passed and amended comprehensive slave codes designed to deny slaves the means of violence, while at the same time protecting the masters in their use of violence against the slaves. The struggle for human space was always fraught with peril, at least for slaves.

Clearly, not all slaves were motivated by the struggle for human dignity or love of their fellows. Some were sinners in a fundamental sense that transcended the rules enacted by the master class to promote their own interests. There were slaves who murdered for the usual reasons—spite, jealousy, greed, revenge—and slaves who stole and cheated, not as an act of resistance but for private gain. And here, added to the normal human distribution of good and evil in any population, there was the devastating psychology of slavery. The white culture devoutly believed in the inferiority of blacks, and the master class worked hard to plant that belief deep in the minds of the people they "owned." This project was aided by the shape of American society. Whites held all the power, wealth, and privilege, while blacks owned virtually nothing—not even themselves, their children, or the right to define and pursue their own interests. Under these circumstances, many blacks could be persuaded that the white view of them was correct. The owners knew that chains on the mind were stronger than shackles on the arms and legs could ever be.

And if not all slaves were blameless, neither were all masters utterly evil. There were kind masters, though kindness in the context of such a heinous criminal enterprise as American slavery must necessarily have a rather shallow meaning. Nevertheless, Richard Allen's owner, Stokeley Sturgis, was an unusually kind man, given the circumstances. He permitted his slaves to participate in religious services and was then himself moved by religion. Inspired by a Methodist preacher who had freed his own slaves, Sturgis set a price for Allen and his brother to purchase their freedom. Some owners allowed, or even encouraged, their slaves to learn how to read. But slavery was for the most part a hard and cruel business, characterized by the slaves' dangerous struggle for dignity.

By the time of the Revolution, all of the Southern states and most of those in the North had codified their laws governing slavery. The earliest laws relating to slavery appeared, like the first drops of a gathering rainstorm, on the books of the Chesapeake tobacco-growing colonies, Virginia and Maryland, in the mid–seventeenth century. The legislatures there and elsewhere passed laws to deal with whatever problems seemed most pressing at any given moment. One early example of such legislative activity is a measure enacted by the Virginia House of Burgesses in 1669.

An Act about the casuall killings of slaves
Whereas the only law in force for the punishment of refractory servants resisting their master, mistress or overseer, cannot be inflicted on negroes [because the punishment was an extension of time in service], Nor the obstinacy of many of them by other than violent meanes supprrest. *Be it enacted and declared by this grand assembly,* if any slave resist his master . . . and by the extremity of the correction should chance to die, that his death shall not be accompted Felony, but the master (or that other person appointed by the master to punish him) be acquit from molestation, since it cannot be presumed that the propensed malice (which alone makes murther Felony) should induce any man to destroy his own estate.

As time passed, legislatures realized that their haphazard manner of legislating on this subject had left them with a confusing mass of enactments that sometimes overlapped, sometimes conflicted, and often left important gaps. The legislation was then streamlined into codes that sought to eliminate these problems. Their main purpose, obviously, was to protect the lives and enhance the wealth of the slave-owning class by controlling the slaves' existence as rigorously as necessary.

The slave codes ultimately came to be something like upside-down bills of rights. The Englishmen in Virginia who owned slaves were jealous of their freedoms and often complained that the king and Parliament intended to reduce them to slavery. Consequently, they spent an enormous amount of their intellectual and political energy defining and asserting the rights they believed were required to keep them free. When it came to their slaves, they proscribed the activities and denied the very rights that the patriots—spearheaded by George Mason—would later decide were vital to protect their own freedoms. Thus the free practice of religion was prohibited, as were freedom of association and freedom of political speech and activity. Freedom to bear arms was obviously out of the question, as were petitions for redress of grievances. The idea of fair trials for blacks was, in the nature of the institution, unthinkable. Cruel and unusual punishment, meanwhile, was an accurate description of the slaves' life circumstances, on top of which they were often subjected to fiendish injury as well.

While the slave codes could stand as a significant retardant to organized rebellion or any meaningful political effort, they could not thwart the most powerful impulses of the human spirit, those toward family, community, and religion. Family formation in the black community was initially impeded by the great imbalance in favor of males in the early shipments of Africans to America. But as the increase in the black population gradually became dependent less upon forced immigration than upon natural increase, the numbers began to balance out, and marriage and family—against enormous odds—became the backbone of the emerging African American culture.

It is difficult to reflect on the powerful, constructive, and nurturing power of relationship and family without concluding that the impediments that slavery threw in the path of marriage were among the most inhumane aspects of that "peculiar institution"—even more inhumane, perhaps, than its inherent raw brutality. Slave owners were at the outset so convinced that blacks were beastlike that they were unable to comprehend the notion of slave marriages. Their law did not sanction such bonds. Some even viewed the idea of slave marriages as high comedy.

To the extent that such unions rose to the level of their attention, the masters reserved all power to control and to rend them. The first power was to withhold approval for a proposed marriage; the second was a blanket policy that made the children of enslaved people the property of the parents' owners. Just to write that sentence is to be struck at a deeper level by how abhorrent these ideas and practices were. The third power, intimately connected to the first, was the right of the master, his family, his friends, and in some circumstances even casual visitors to impose themselves sexually on any female slave, whether or not she happened to be married. Of course, many slave masters were repulsed by such behavior, but many more practiced it, as the great variety of skin colors in the contemporary African American population attests.

Sometimes sexual relations between masters and their slaves were long-lasting and filled with affection. That was apparently the case, for example, between Thomas Jefferson's father-in-law, John Wayles, and his slave Elizabeth Hemings. Wayles had children both by his wife and by his slave; his daughter Martha Wayles, who married Jefferson, thus had a half-sister, Sally Hemings. Sally, who was said to be beautiful and to resemble her half-sister, came to be owned by Jefferson by inheritance after Wayles's death.

The mixed-race Sally Hemings presents a stunning example of whites' impulse to reduce blacks (or even quarter-blacks: Sally's mother was half white) to something below full human status in order to protect their racial fantasies. Hemings first came to public notice when James Callender, a disappointed office-seeker and muckraking journalist, published allegations that Jefferson kept a slave concubine and had had several children by her. Callender asserted that it was well known in the environs of Monticello that there were a number of light-skinned slave children who looked like Jefferson running around his plantation. Jefferson himself never answered these charges, but others mounted a nearly two-century-long effort to deny them and discredit both the people and the evidence that supported the story.

The family story told by the white Jefferson family—his daughter and his grandson—was that the Jefferson-like slave children were the products of Hemings's relationship with one of Jefferson's nephews (either Peter or Samuel Carr). The Hemings family story was told by Sally's son Madison in a memoir he published in the *Pike County* (Ohio) *Republican* on March 13, 1873. Madison Hemings reported that his mother had told him Jefferson was his father and the father of his four siblings, three of whom—Beverly, Harriet, and Eston—had survived with him into adulthood. He recounted particulars of their lives, as well as details of life at Monticello and his recollections of his father.

The reigning arbiters of this dispute were Jefferson's admiring white biographers, who for more than a century dismissed Madison Hemings's story as the attempt of a pitiful old colored man to grab some measure of prestige. They credited the white Jeffersons' family story because it coincided with what they believed they *knew* of Jefferson's character. They persisted in this belief even after Dumas Malone, Jefferson's most celebrated biographer, established that Jefferson, though frequently away from home, had been with Sally in Paris (in the case of the child conceived there) or at Monticello nine months before each of her deliveries. A moment's thought yields the conclusion that in order for the nephew story to be true, one of the Carr brothers would have had to force himself on Sally—repeatedly—virtually in the presence of his uncle.

It was only the cumulative weight of the research of the historian Fawn Brodie, author of *Thomas Jefferson: An Intimate History;* the work of the novelist Barbara Chase-Riboud, author of *Sally Hemings;* the persistence of oral traditions in many strands of black families who trace their lines back to Hemings and Jefferson; and finally the efforts of author Annette Gordon-Reed that prompted comparative DNA testing of, among others, Jefferson's uncle

Field Jefferson, a number of male Jefferson and Carr descendants, and one of the male Hemings descendants. The tests established that Eston Hemings and his descendants were descended from a male Jefferson. The only candidates alive at the time of Eston's birth were Jefferson's uncle, his brother, and Jefferson himself. The DNA testing demolished the Carr brothers' scenario because they were the offspring of Jefferson's sister. Jefferson's proximity to Sally, her likeness to her half-sister—his beloved deceased wife —and Madison Hemings's recollections all point to a strong circumstantial probability that Jefferson was the father of Eston Hemings, the only one of Sally Hemings's male children who had locatable male descendants.

The real story here is the amount of energy that was put into denying the Hemings-Jefferson connection, and the easy contempt that was employed to dismiss Madison Hemings's straightforward—even pedestrian—testimony about who he was and what his mother had told him about where he came from. The elements that sustained the white Jefferson family story as *the truth* were that relatively few whites could believe that this American founder could possibly have *debased* himself by lying repeatedly with a person who was even half black; that white people's versions of the way things were *are* the way things were; that black people's versions of the way things were are discredited at the source and thus may be discounted without any attempt at analysis; and that white scholarly experts can take up their writing materials and create truth simply by writing over and through the reality of existence as experienced by black people.

It all adds up to a very complex strategy for removing blacks from the rank of humans. If you extinguish blacks' voices, you eliminate their ability to validate the realities of their lives. That leaves the field open for white fantasies to become truth, as with the fantasy that blacks are so debased that there are some activities in which they clearly cannot have participated (such as shaping a country or making babies with a hero), and so far from entering "into a state of society" that white words and wishes alone can define their truths. We have seen this in many areas, for example in the racist jurisprudence practiced by Justices Tucker and Taney.

Many whites have long believed that blacks who try to prove that they are descendants of famous whites are desperately seeking status. What blacks really seem to be saying is that we are human, we count, we have been here, and we are tired of the lies.

However you slice the Monticello story—whether you believe the Madison Hemings version or the daughter's and grandson's story about the Carr brothers—it is clear that some white slaveholder, either Thomas Jefferson himself or Samuel or Peter Carr, repeatedly took advantage of the master-slave relationship to derive sexual pleasure and perhaps some human comfort from a woman owned by Thomas Jefferson. Whether the father was Jefferson or a nephew, the sexual usage of Sally Hemings for almost forty years, beginning when she was a young teenager, was made possible by one fact: Jefferson's "ownership" of her. One can wonder, Who is fully human in this situation, and who is not?

While white men could usually use their power to take slave women with impunity, the love that black husbands had for their wives sometimes complicated matters. In *The World They Made Together: Black and White Values in Eighteenth-Century Virginia,* Mechal Sobel recounts one such story, narrated by a fellow called Old Dick:

> Old Dick tells us that young Thomas Sutherland was murdered by a slave, whose wife he had apparently taken with violence. Sutherland was reputed to have been *mighty ficious when he got among the negur wenches. He used to say that a likely negur wench was fit to be a Queen; and I forget how many Queens he had among the girls on the plantations. . . . The young 'Squire did not live long. He was for a short life and a merry one. He was killed by a drunken negur man, who found him over-ficious with his wife. The negur man was hanged alive upon a gibbet. It was in the middle of summer; the sun was full upon him; the negur lolled out his tongue, his eyes seemed starting from their sockets, and for three long days his only cry was Water! Water! Water!*

The story of the "drunken negur man"'s revenge is instructive. His reaction is within the range of behavior to which we might expect a "normal civilized" man to be driven if some "merry" lout violently defiled his wife. It certainly belies the idea that blacks were too brutish to form strong marital attachments.

But in the end it is a cautionary tale: black men were ultimately powerless to defend the honor of their wives. The power of "civilization" could be counted on to be surely and swiftly executed in such cases.

Even crueler than invading a marriage, however, was depriving slave parents of the power to protect their children. Their children were *owned* by the master. Mary Prince, a slave, wrote about seeking her parents' protection from a brutal master. After being beaten until she could bear no more, Mary escaped to the plantation where her mother was held. But that poor soul could only give her child refuge in a cave and spirit food to her surreptitiously. Her father, a slave at still another place, learned of Mary's suffering and came and took her back to her master. Mary recalled:

> Oh I was loth, loth to go back; but as there was no remedy, I was obliged to submit.
>
> When we got home, my poor father said to Cap. I——, "Sir, I am sorry that my child should be forced to run away from her owner; but the treatment she has received is enough to break her heart. The sight of her wounds has nearly broke mine.—I entreat you, for the love of God, to forgive her for running away, and that you will be a kind master to her in future." Capt. I—— said I was used as well as I deserved, and that I ought to be punished for running away. I then took courage and said that I could stand the floggings no longer; that I was weary of my life, and therefore I had run away to my mother; but that mothers could only weep and mourn over their children, they could not save them from cruel masters—from the whip, the rope, and the cow-skin. He told me to hold my tongue and go about my work, or he would find a way to settle me. He did not, however, flog me that day.

As the father of two daughters myself, I shrivel inside when I think of powerless girls and women being forced to submit, knowing that their families could give them no help whatsoever. Similarly, I find it almost impossible to imagine the pain inflicted on a parent when a member of the master class took a sexual fancy to a slave child. The contemplation of parental powerlessness in the face of punishments visited upon children by means of the "whip, the rope and the cow-skin" is likewise soul-shredding.

Finally, families were held hostage to the whim and fortune of the master. They could be ripped asunder by his need, for example, to sell off some slaves to raise ready cash. Mary Prince tells of the master who kept her mother while selling Mary and her siblings because he needed money to get married: "Oh dear! I cannot bear to think of that day,—it is too much.—It recalls the great grief that filled my heart, and the woeful thoughts that passed to and fro through my mind, whilst listening to the pitiful words of my poor mother, weeping for the loss of her children."

Mary's mother had borne the burden of preparing her three daughters for the sale, dressing them in new clothes—"shrouding them," she called it—and orchestrating their leave-taking from the people and places that had provided what little comfort was available to slave children. From that moment of sadness, the little family dropped into a pit of deepest despair as the mother delivered her children to the slave market. These were Mary's observations:

> Did one of the many by-standers, who were looking at us so carelessly, think of the pain that wrung the hearts of the negro woman and her young ones? No, no! They were not all bad, I dare say, but slavery hardens white people's hearts towards the blacks; and many of them regard our grief—though their light words fell like cayenne on the fresh wounds of our hearts.

She was led to the center of the marketplace, where the inspection began.

> I was soon surrounded by strange men, who examined and handled me in the same manner that a butcher would a calf or a lamb he was about to purchase, and who talked about my shape and size in like words—as if I could no more understand their meaning than the dumb beasts. I was then put up for sale. . . .
> I then saw my sisters led forth, and sold to different owners; so that we had not the sad satisfaction of being partners in bondage. . . . It was a sad parting; one went one way, one another, and our poor mammy went home with nothing.

Families could also be parted if the master decided to make a gift of a slave or two or by will at his death. They could be parted if the master's son, say, decided to pull up stakes and seek his fortune in the West with the help of a trusty slave—leaving that slave's family behind. Slaves were only property, after all; their pain could be ignored. To ease their guilt, whites invented and clung to the idea that blacks had no family feeling.

Despite all these crippling constraints, blacks *did* marry, and forged enormously strong family ties. Stories are legion of black men who bought their own freedom and then the freedom of their wives and children; of blacks who went without sleep and took long nocturnal trips to squeeze in marital visits in the short time given to them between sundown and sunup; of black families like Mary Prince's, heartbroken when they were split up and sold. Some masters noticed the pain that forced separations caused and stopped selling slaves. Even George Washington, who began as a strict master, ultimately recognized the inhumanity inherent in the sale of slaves. In 1794 he wrote to a friend, "I am principled agt. selling negros, as you would do catle in the market."

Then there are the freedom stories. At the end of the Civil War, blacks were so impoverished, so illiterate, and for the most part so lacking in skills that freedom meant little more to them than the ability to leave the place to which they had been tethered by slavery. The postwar records are replete with poignant tales of blacks who took to the roads and retraced their paths back to the plantations from which they had been sold, in search of the families they had lost.

There were surely blacks who were so battered by the system of slavery that they became sexually promiscuous or irresponsible as parents. There were surely some who internalized the contempt that the master class had for tenderness in slaves, so that they became calloused and brutalizing people themselves—users of others and abusers of the best in themselves. Unquestionably, slavery did its damage in this area, as in many others. But it could not extinguish all tenderness or all family feeling. Indeed, for many blacks, slavery sharpened such feelings and deepened the obligations of caring and love that naturally flow from them. Nevertheless, the casualties and the pain that paved the way to the strengths of so many black families in freedom also constitute one of the worst elements in the terrible story of American slavery.

In spite of slavery, and perhaps because of the powerful human impulse to survive, love, and nurture, blacks built strong communities on the plantations. The space required for family and community to develop was created by the tension between what the masters desired and expected and the fact that slaves were humans, not machines. The masters provided less-than-adequate shelter, food, and clothing, and the slaves brought in the tobacco, cotton, grain, and sugar cane. In return for their labor, the slaves could hope for at most a few moments in the evening and the chance to raise a bit of extra food. They made the most of the night. The night was made for family, community, religious practice, gaiety, and love. It was a time for renewing kinship and community ties, a time when people sneaked from plantation to plantation to visit their spouses or other loved ones.

In the end, there was space for black community building because the system in Virginia rested on the slave. One writer has quoted others to make the point: " 'The custom of the country is such,' wrote a Baptist minister, 'that without slaves, a man's children stand but a poor chance to marry in reputation,' or even, according to another commentator, 'to appear in polite company.' "

Slaves understood their leverage. People so essential to the economy, to the prestige and the psychic health of the master class, could not be denied living space to form communities if they were clever enough to force the issue without directly challenging the institution and bringing down destruction upon their own heads. The slaves *were* that clever, and thus they compelled their masters to yield the space they needed.

The pace of this process quickened as the revolutionary crisis approached. Because the mood of the master was a vital part of their environment, slaves were quick to get wind of the revolutionary impulse as it began to stir in the 1760s. When whites demonstrated in Charleston against the Stamp Act, a group of slaves caught the spirit and marched through the streets shouting, "Liberty! Liberty!" It was a sight that sent shivers up and down the spines of slave owners in that colony.

When the budding rebellion moved to the streets, blacks joined the mobs. Crispus Attucks, a freed slave, became the first American to die in the Revolution when he was cut down by a British bullet in the Boston Massacre. Thus, from the beginning, the American Revolution swept up both white *and* black Americans in its spirit and in its bloodshed.

Blacks heard the cry of freedom as white patriots inveighed against the attempts of the king to reduce them to "slavery" and submitted their own natural-rights petitions for freedom. Some fought at Lexington and Concord and Bunker Hill. Others believed Lord Dunmore's promise to free them if they would join him. There were undoubtedly some blacks, such as Attucks and Salem Poor, a hero at Bunker Hill, who were genuine American patriots, offended by the overbearing king and his Redcoats. And there were doubtless still others who were just as dedicated to freedom but whose loyalty ran to self, kin, and community, and who wanted freedom any way they could get it.

And so by the end of the war blacks made up 20 percent of Washington's armies, leaving the fields and plantations by the thousands as they sought their freedom behind British lines. Blacks had every imaginable experience in the war short of commanding white troops. Many died of malaria contracted in the swamps as they followed Lord Dunmore, Virginia's last colonial governor. One black man, Billy Lee, served at General Washington's side and eased his life in every wartime setting from Cambridge through Valley Forge to Yorktown. Others served as infantrymen, as watermen, or as slaves doing the heavy lifting of war.

Still others acted as scouts and spies. In 1781, for example, a slave named Saul Matthews stole into the British garrison near Portsmouth and gathered important information that would ultimately enable American troops to take the garrison. He would distinguish himself again in Norfolk and would be accorded the highest praise by General Nathaniel Greene. Perhaps Saul Matthews and others like him were successful as spies precisely because white men could not imagine being fooled by blacks.

Stories of blacks who participated in the Revolution demonstrate, more than anything, that black people, whether slave or free, were surely not inert or content with the conditions imposed upon them by white Americans. Nor were they viewed that way by either the British or the white Americans themselves. Some were sufficiently stirred by the patriots' cause to risk their lives fighting for it *and* for their freedom, while others cared so much for their freedom that they took the enormous chance of fleeing their masters *and then* endangering their lives again in the war. Among the latter may well have been the thirty slaves who took the opportunity afforded by the war to flee Monticello.

Elizabeth Freeman, a Massachusetts slave, caught the revolutionary spirit in her own way. After being struck on the arm and burned by a hot shovel wielded by her master, she asked a young lawyer to present the case for her freedom based on the bill of rights contained in the state constitution. Freeman, who would bear the burn scar for the rest of her life, said she had overheard conversations about the bill of rights while serving meals and had concluded that its assertion that all men were born free and equal meant she could no longer be held in slavery. After her lawyer, Theodore Sedgwick, made the case, the court agreed with Freeman and ruled that the new constitution had indeed abolished slavery in the commonwealth of Massachusetts. Years later, when Elizabeth Freeman died, Sedgwick would eulogize her as a "practical refutation of the imagined superiority of our race to hers."

There is no question that the Revolution gave Americans an opportunity to encounter one another across racial lines as they had never done before. It enabled blacks to reach for freedom in ways that had been impossible during the colonial years. And many found in the crimped and throttling mold of slavery a crack large enough to allow them to realize a fuller range of their human potential. Among the most telling of such human activities were the simple and powerful petitions that blacks addressed to the white patriots, asking for the logical justice of their doing unto their black fellow Americans as they would have the British do unto them. Another consequence of great significance was that some white Americans, like General Nathaniel Greene and Theodore Sedgwick, were given the opportunity to transcend the stifling bonds of color identity that their culture had forced upon their spirits, and to see clearly the full human dimensions of those of their fellow Americans who were black. Nevertheless, on the whole, America had become a country in which a good part of white self-esteem flowed simply from *not being black*. In order for that psychological prop to work, whites had to convince themselves that black subordination was in the natural order of things, rather than an arbitrary hierarchy imposed on blacks because of racism, greed, and superior power. That construct was to become a powerful engine in the American mechanism of racism.

For blacks, in addition to the terrible physical and cultural deprivations inflicted upon them, there were enormous psychic costs. The most damaging of these was the internalization of the constant cultural message that they were inferior to whites in every respect. Just as self-love can be enriching beyond understanding (as, for example, in the case of George Washington), self-hatred can be the most destructive of human feelings. Obviously, the selling of slavery to the culture necessarily involved the selling of a huge amount of destructive self-hatred to black people. Over the centuries, this has resulted in the mangling of far too many souls of black folks by that terrible psychic force.

By the time of the Revolution, the families of many blacks and whites had been in the colonies for generations. From the noblest characters, such as Salem Poor, Elizabeth Freeman, and George Washington, to the most brutal slave owner and the nastiest, most dishonorable slave, they had been forged in the culture that *all* the immigrants to North America had created, in concert with the people who were already here when they came. One group was artificially subordinated, another—the totality of Native American peoples—was being hounded to the edges of "civilization," and the third was artificially inflated. But they were linked by their common life on the land they shared. They were Americans.

The two black Americans who would found the Free African Society, Absalom Jones and Richard Allen, were among those not affected by self-hatred. They were at work in Philadelphia in the spring of 1787 as the delegates to the Constitutional Convention were arriving to do *their* work. Jones had been born a slave in Sussex County, Delaware, in 1746, and Allen had been born in slavery in Philadelphia fourteen years later. Both men had labored hard and saved religiously to buy their freedom, and Jones's wife had purchased hers as well. By 1787 both men were prominent members of Philadelphia's free black community. That year they and other blacks had worshiped with white Methodists and become acutely aware of the second-class status they were accorded even by their coreligionists. When they attempted to establish an institution of worship for themselves, they were thwarted by the white Methodists. Thus temporarily diverted, they established a nondenominational organization, the Free African Society, to promote the interests of black people.

As historians Kaplan and Kaplan describe it,

> the opening sentence of [the society's] Articles of Association had the feeling of a great beginning: "We the free Africans and their descendants . . . do unanimously agree, for the benefit of each other . . ." And the preamble rang out:
>
> "Whereas, Absalom Jones and Richard Allen, two men of the African race, who, for their religious life and conversation have obtained a good report among men, from a love to the people of their complexion whom they beheld with sorrow . . . often communed together . . . in order to form some kind of religious society, but there being too few to be found under the like concern, and those who were, differed in their religious sentiments; with these circumstances they labored for some time, till it was proposed, after a serious communication of sentiments, that a society should be formed without regard to religious tenets, provided, the persons lived an orderly and sober life, in order to support one another in sickness, and for the benefit of their widows and fatherless children."

Both Allen and Jones were possessed of enormous will and discipline. Each was a bear for hard work, and each was blessed with a master unusual in being willing to sell a slave his freedom. Both were devout.

While he was still enslaved, Allen had deepened his religious understanding in the same way as thousands of slaves before him: he left the plantation and attended church meetings in the forest. Writing about this period later, Allen recalled, "Our neighbors, seeing that our master indulged us with the privilege of attending meetings once in two weeks, said that Stokeley's negroes would soon ruin him; and so my brother and myself held a council together . . . so that it should not be said that religion made us worse servants; we would work night and day to get our crops forward. . . . At length, our master was convinced that religion made slaves better and not worse, and often boasted of his slaves for their honesty and industry."

Allen was free by the time of the Revolution and was working and preaching. He drove a wagon during the war and continued to speak the word of God; by war's end he had become a traveling preacher who often pushed himself beyond his own physical limits. Jones and his wife, meanwhile, had worked hard enough in their freedom to become owners of rental property; they were already pillars of the Philadelphia black community when Allen arrived there. The two men would become longtime collaborators, with Jones going on to found the first black Episcopal church in North America, and Allen to establish the African Methodist Episcopal Church, the first black denomination in the United States. These two men who had struggled up out of slavery would thus lay much of the foundation of the American black church, an entity that would serve as the backbone of black life in this country down through our own time. This they did with intelligence, idealism, spirituality, self-respect, dignity, and love for their fellow men. They surely answered Clay Hopper's query, 160 years before it was put to Branch Rickey. Allen and Jones were unquestionably full human beings. And like Washington and Jefferson, they were American heroes of enormous distinction.

CHAPTER 5

A Blood American

He is the father of everyone and he lives in the sky. He will come
through the clouds one day and deliver his black children into
freedom.

My great-great-grandmother ———— Jeffries

We hold these truths to be self-evident; that all men are created
equal; that they are endowed by their Creator with certain inalienable rights; that among these are life, liberty and the pursuit of
happiness. . . .

The Second Continental Congress and Thomas Jefferson

Four score and seven years ago our fathers brought forth on this
continent, a new nation, conceived in Liberty, and dedicated to
the proposition that all men are created equal.

Now we are engaged in a great civil war, testing whether
that nation, or any nation so conceived and so dedicated can long
endure. . . .

Abraham Lincoln

A few years ago, I visited the Cape Coast Castle, on the Gulf of
Guinea in Ghana. Although I had made a number of trips to the
continent over three decades—to East, Central, North, and
southern Africa—I had never been to that bulge in the landmass
nearest America, from which so many Africans had been shipped
west. During my first few days in Ghana, I was stunned by how
many people looked familiar to me. Waiting for a luncheon to
start at the State Visitors' House, I idly glanced at a painting of a

Ghanaian funeral scene and was shocked to see a mourner who looked very much like my father. One of our guides reminded me of one of my daughters, and a woman I glimpsed in a market resembled one of my aunts. I had experienced no similar sense of recognition on any of my earlier trips to Africa. It was clear to me that I had found one of the places of my family's origin and that here in Ghana I was surrounded by distant cousins.

This discovery was still seeping into my soul a few days later, when our conference broke for a trip to see the Cape Coast Castle. This imposing structure, on a promontory above the ocean, had served simultaneously as a fort, a warehouse, a prison, and a shipping dock. The commandant's rooms were spacious and kept aired by fresh breezes from the ocean. Not far from his apartment was a large room that we were told had normally been an officers' dining room but on special occasions had doubled as a grand ballroom. Its high ceilings, its generous dimensions, and the lovely promenades just outside made it easy to imagine gay and splendid affairs' being held inside.

Down below, things were less splendid. There was a big courtyard where the soldiers had formed up in ranks and paraded around, as they do in forts. But this wasn't an ordinary fort, and the more critical use of the open space was for sorting, cleaning, showing, and selling the merchandise that was processed through the castle for more than two centuries. We were shown peepholes through which white men could examine, unobserved, the black captives as they were brought to the fort. After inspecting the new arrivals and making their purchases—and perhaps picking out some likely-looking women for concubines—the traders would mark their captives and dispatch them to the dungeons to await the arrival of the slave ships.

After being told these things, we were taken down to the dungeons. On the way, I noticed a door off the courtyard marked with a skull and crossbones. I asked about it and was told that the room behind the door had been used as an execution chamber: any prisoner who committed a serious breach of the rules would be shut up in there. The room was as airtight as sixteenth-century construction could make it, and the prisoner would be locked in, denied food and water, and left to die of dehydration, starvation, or asphyxiation—whichever came first.

The dungeon had been hacked out of ground that sloped down toward the ocean. The place was dim, with only a couple of small windows, up high. There was one little trough cut into the sloping ground, which we were told was for urine. Solid waste was a more difficult problem, apparently; people might be held for weeks before their ship came in, during which time they would be taken out periodically and splashed off and then sent back down to await their fates. As we walked farther down the slope inside the dungeon, we were funneled by the contours of the place toward a door. When it was opened, bright sunlight exploded into the dimness, but the opening was so narrow that an adult had to squeeze through sideways. The captives were sent out naked and made to feel utterly powerless as they were extruded through the "door of no return" into the blinding brightness. They then stumbled or were driven onto the stinking slavers that would take them on the Middle Passage to the far outposts of Western civilization.

Pushing through that door, I felt faint and found it a little hard to breathe as I tried to cope with the power and the pain of the history I was feeling. I was sure to a moral certainty that some of those who had contributed to the streams of blood that were pounding through my veins at that moment had been forced through that very door two to three centuries earlier. I stood there facing the ocean, with my back to the continent of Africa, and thought about my African cousins and ancestors as I peered out at the horizon, where the ocean curved toward the Americas. And I knew that no matter how deeply these African memories or the vitality of my African cousins might move me, somewhere over that curve, on the other side of that ocean, was my home. The centuries had done their work. I understood absolutely that I was fully an American.

I thought then about my great-grandfather Charles Wood, a Virginian who was born a hundred years after George Washington and a hundred years before me. He married a woman named

Percidia, a Cherokee, and together they had thirteen children, including my mother's mother, Amy Brown Wood, who helped to
raise me. Charles Wood is said to have been very active in sending
people to freedom on the underground railroad, from his town,
Burgess Store, in Northumberland County, Virginia. I have a
photograph of him and also some letters he wrote. The picture
shows a distinguished-looking, light-skinned man with a neatly
trimmed beard, dressed in quite formal clothing. His handwriting
is copy-book clear, and his use of English excellent.

We are told that he was a freeman who worked in the postal
service, and there is some half-remembered family lore that attributes his education from childhood to the patronage of a white
woman in the community. I have always wondered how this black
man got his freedom and his light skin. Even in the 1600s, there
were a few free blacks in Virginia. Once, when my family and I
visited the replica of the Jamestown settlement, our guide paused
in his remarks about the seventeenth-century inhabitants of the
colony, looked at my wife, my daughter Elizabeth, and me (the
only blacks in the group of tourists), and said, a bit triumphantly, I
thought, "There were blacks here then. Blacks are among the first
families of Virginia."

I suppose it is just barely possible that my great-grandfather
Wood was descended from very early free blacks, but it seems
more likely that the family freedom came later—through fighting in the Revolution, perhaps? Or was Charles Wood light and
free because he was the child of a slave and a white person—was
his lightness the result of an owner's forcing himself on a slave
woman? Was the white woman who took an interest in him a relative, or simply a kind slave-owning woman who saw promise in
the half-black child and so educated and freed him? Could she
have been his mother? Whatever the explanation, there surely had
been a long journey of genes and circumstances from some door
of no return to the light and educated man born thirty-three years
before Lee surrendered at Appomattox.

But the painting I saw in the Ghanaian State Visitors' House
and the people I "recognized" on the street in Accra did not look
like the Wood side of my family. They looked like Wilkins peo-

ple—like my father, Earl, and his sister, Armeda, and his brother, Roy (and like my daughters, who both look something like their great-aunt Armeda). A few years before he died, my uncle Roy published an autobiography, *Standing Fast,* in which he pushed as deeply into the American story of this formerly African family as he could. Thanks to the generosity of his literary executors, I am able to share a gift that few black families have: a published account of our family in slavery and early freedom. I will quote liberally here from this part of his book because what he wrote is precisely relevant to my own feelings about America. Moreover, I hope that this extract will motivate some to read my uncle's book in its entirety. Uncle Roy wrote this:

> I was not born in Mississippi, but my story begins there all the same, deep in the rolling hill country of northern Mississippi. If you travel far enough into the heart of those hills, not far south of Holly Springs you will come upon an old dirt road wandering off the black-top highway that races on to Senatobia. The dusty road goes down a dip, winds around a slight curve, then comes to a stop right at the front door of a little country church called Beverly Chapel, a spare wooden building painted white and filled with pine pews. There is no stained glass in the windows, no steeple atop the roof; only a gnarled bell tower of cypress poles weathered hard by the sun and rain stands out front. On Sundays an old iron bell used to clang from the bell tower's rickety crossbeam, calling black people from the farms and countryside to worship. The bell is gone now. Most days the only sounds that break the peaceful quiet of the place are the soft drone of honeybees, the lilting call of bobwhites, and the chirp of small blackbirds nesting in a hole above the weather-beaten church door. A footpath bordered with wild daisies and tangled weeds threads its way to the Negro cemetery out back, where my grandfather and grandmother, Asberry and Emma Wilkins, lie buried. A tall stand of cypresses overlooks their graves. They have no other markers: no headstones, no dates or epitaphs carved for the ages, nothing. My grandparents were slaves—and the soil of Mississippi has swallowed them as indifferently as it produced them in the 1850s, ten years before Abraham Lincoln set them free.
>
> Lost among the untended graves, my mother is also buried out behind Beverly Chapel. Except for good fortune I, too, might have

disappeared into the earth there. This particular burying ground holds the first truth about my family: go back two generations and our freedom vanishes; go back any farther and the family itself disappears. We have been Americans for well over two hundred years, but for much of that time we were a family without a name and for most practical purposes without a country. Up to the time of the Civil War the branches of our family tree rustled with bills of sale, not birth certificates. We were sold by sex, age, and weight, not by name, and as a consequence of this loathsome traffic in human flesh, my ancestors from the third generation back are as lost as any missing tribe of Israel.

The few fragments of our early history that survive were handed down by Grandfather Wilkins, a tall man with skin as black and lustrous as polished ebony. He had deep brown eyes that burned with intelligence and a steady warmth, and his sinewy arms could keep a span of mules plowing a straight furrow all day or tuck a protesting grandchild gently into bed at sundown. He had received his education at the end of a hoe and an eleven-foot cotton sack.

During the winter of 1914, when I was thirteen years old, I spent Christmas on his little farm outside Holly Springs. . . . It was very warm for December, and the townspeople of Holly Springs shot off fireworks in honor of Christ's birth, almost as if they were celebrating the Fourth of July. Grandfather Wilkins lived just across the road and down a small hill from Beverly Chapel. . . . He was a tenant farmer, hardworking, sober, thrifty, up first from slavery, then from the misery of sharecropping. His own people called him a good Christian man. The white folks of Holly Springs called him a "good nigger": that is to say, a black man who did nothing to expose the gap between the pretensions of the white South to Christian virtue and the unholy way most white Southerners treated their black brothers and sisters all year round. . . .

Grandfather Wilkins owned a mule named Kel, a few clothes, his tools, and his Bible. The relics of his past were equally meager. The name of his father, which has survived only as an illegible scrawl on a death certificate buried in the archives of Mississippi, appears to have been Mound Jeffries. . . . Great-grandfather Jeffries, a field hand, had jumped the broomstick, marrying my great-grandmother, whose name is now lost. Their boy child was strong and very black, two credentials that fitted him perfectly for the place the white folks of Marshall County [Mississippi] had reserved for him: down at the bottom. . . .

A small child could not have started out in life with much more against him. The United States Constitution itself considered him only three-fifths of a human being, the fractional representation in the human race that was granted to determine the number of white Mississippians who would fight year after year in the Congress of the United States to keep him a slave. It was a hard time. But at night the North Star twinkled brightly in the sky, showing him the way to New England and Canada, where blacks could be free. And in the slave quarters after dark, his mother would lie by his side telling him stories about an all-powerful, loving God.

"He is the father of everyone and he lives in the sky," she told him one night. "He will come through the clouds one day and deliver his black children into freedom." . . .

Grandfather Wilkins was tormented by a child's relentless literalism, by questions that would not leave him alone: Was God white or black? Was one side of God white and the other side black? How could God say He loved black people when He allowed them to be slaves? . . .

[At the end of the Civil War,] the Union victory didn't liberate the slaves of Marshall County overnight. . . . One day in the summer of 1865, the overseers herded Grandfather Wilkins and the other slaves on his plantation into a large group at the edge of one of the cotton fields. Just at noon, the master came out of his house and walked slowly down to the fields. When he reached the waiting slaves, he studied his boots for a few minutes. Finally, he looked up and spoke to them.

"The Yankee soldiers say y'all free. I don't hafta feed you or take such good care of you anymore—unless you want to stay on the plantation and keep on working for me."

For a moment there was silence. Then, softly, one of the older slaves began to sing. The words of one of the old Sorrow Songs suddenly full of joy rose and rolled across the plantation:

> *"Didn't my Lord deliver Daniel,*
> *Deliver Daniel, deliver Daniel?*
> *Didn't my Lord deliver Daniel?*
> *An' why not every man?"*

One by one the other slaves began to sing, and when they finished they fell to their knees out in that cotton field and gave thanks to God—my great-grandmother's God of deliverance. Grandfather Wilkins had doubted. But on that day of jubilation, it looked as if his mother had been right all along.

At the end of the Civil War, my great-grandfather Wilkins—who was only fourteen at the time, not much older than my uncle Roy was when he visited his grandparents—decided to keep on working for his old master. He lived out the rest of his life in Holly Springs, first as a semi-slave during Reconstruction and the time of the Redeemers and then as a poor tenant farmer. He married Emma, a former house slave for a woman in town, and they had five children, including William DeWitte Wilkins, who as a young man was called Willie. Willie married a schoolteacher named Mayfield Edmundson in June 1900. Soon after their wedding, the groom beat up a smirking white man who had ordered him off a country road near Holly Springs. That was a lynching offense in Mississippi in those days, but a good white friend helped my great-grandfather save his son. Uncle Roy tells it this way:

> Late that afternoon, a worried white friend for whom Grandfather Wilkins did chores came calling at the farm.
> "Uncle Asberry," he said, "you better get that boy Willie out of town. He's making trouble for both of us. There's nothing I can do for him. He's heading for a lynching, sure."

That night my great-grandfather bundled up Willie and his bride and hustled them up to Memphis and the Illinois Central train that would take them to St. Louis, where their first child, Roy, would be born the following summer. Two years later their daughter, Armeda, was born, followed in late 1905 by my father, Earl. Before my father was a year old, my grandmother contracted tuberculosis and died. Her sister, Elizabeth, acceded to her wish that her children not be raised in Mississippi and took them home with her to Minnesota. My grandmother Mayfield Wilkins—called Sweetie by her friends and family—was shipped back to Holly Springs for burial in the little cemetery next to Beverly Chapel.

Many years after Uncle Roy visited that quiet, run-down, but very pretty cemetery, I made my own pilgrimage there and stood alone in that place where my grandmother was buried in 1906, my great-grandfather Asberry in 1917, and my great-grandmother Emma in 1922, with no stone to mark any of their lives and struggles. By the time of my visit, the entire older generation of my Wilkins line was gone—Armeda buried in Minnesota in the mid-1920s, my father buried in Missouri in 1941, Grandpa Willie buried in Missouri in the late 1950s, and Roy buried in 1981 out on Long Island, not so far from the place where F. Scott Fitzgerald set his brilliant rumination about the American dream. I stood there in the Beverly Chapel cemetery and thought about those buried within feet of me, about my great-great-grandparents Jeffries, probably buried no more than a few miles away, and then about all of the rest of my ancestors from all the generations buried in other places all over the American earth.

I remembered that Mississippi visit and all of my dead as I stood at the foot of the Cape Coast Castle. And I remembered the other lines of my American ancestry as well. The Cherokee strand ran back much much further than the Jamestown settlement, and the black and white strands went back at least two centuries, maybe even three. A lot of blood and toil, pain and joy had roiled through the veins that ultimately flowed down to me in the mid–twentieth century. A lot of living, suffering, and triumph in the building of America had been experienced by the people who through the generations had dropped their genes to me. Their American lives had surely made America mine. For me to aspire to be something other than American would be to renounce all their contributions to this country, all their struggles for space in which to live their lives, all the things they built, all the wealth they created, all the love they passed down the generations that came to me. Among other things, it would be a renunciation of Charles Wood's fine and dangerous work in smuggling Virginia slaves to freedom, of the comfort Great-great-grandmother ———— Jeffries (her first name is lost to us) tried to give to her little boy as he grew up in slavery, of Great-grandfather Asberry's hustling my grandparents to safety just ahead of the lynch mob, of my father's excellent journalism and my mother's exemplary civic and civil rights career, and of the Medal of Freedom Uncle Roy earned by helping to lead the fight for civil rights all of his adult life.

Mound Jeffries and his wife, my great-great-grandmother, reduced to a nameless vessel for the production of labor, are as far back as I can reach in my family toward the Cape Coast Castle. As Uncle Roy observed, when you push farther back, the family disappears. But though ———— Jeffries wasn't free, we know that she wasn't entirely owned, either. She reserved her soul for herself and her family, and that soul—whatever else there was in her life, whatever glories or failures she experienced as a human being—that soul had love and faith and hope. This was her human essence, down deep inside her, beyond the reach of her "owners" but at the ready and available for her family. With them she was fully human, fully American.

She certainly wasn't an African anymore. She didn't look back toward an African past, but rather focused her gaze forward, toward a life of freedom in America—a freedom that she promised her son he would have. Her idea of a better life was a better *American* life. That was a remarkable notion—a remarkable faith—for an enslaved black woman to have in Mississippi in 1855 or 1856. Part of that faith was obviously rooted in religion: God would make things right. But the definition of what was right—freedom—and the plausibility of the yearning were both rooted in something more earthly, more human, more American. They were rooted in the social and political physics of freedom, set in motion by the founding generation to which Mason, Washington, Jefferson, and Madison, despite their slaveholdings, made massive contributions.

Nevertheless, when I think about the misery that American slavery inflicted on so many millions of black Americans for so many generations, and when I personalize that misery in ———— and Mound Jeffries and in Asberry and Emma Wilkins, I feel a rising rage that men so distinguished and so powerful could have been so timid about using that power in the cause of freedom for blacks and justice for America. I want to take those four lives—as emblems of millions of others like them—and push them in the faces of those four founders and say, "Look at the pain you might have avoided and the potential you might have liberated had you had the capacity to care for human beings like these as deeply as you cared for yourselves and for people like you." But that's the rub, of course. They couldn't because they were morally crippled by their culture and politically shackled by the grating chain that snaked through the new republic and diminished every life it touched.

And yet each of the founding Virginia fathers was able to achieve enough moral growth in his lifetime to contribute to the accumulating weight that would lead to freedom at least for the Jeffrieses' little boy and for Emma, the girl he would one day marry. The four founders might have freed all their slaves in their lifetimes and thereby lost enough status, wealth, and leisure to be rendered anonymous. But financially—and probably psychically as well—they were incapable of such sacrifices.

Great-great-grandmother Jeffries knew that her soul and her son's could not be owned. And he took her gifts in the way she intended, so that when the time came, and Asberry was a free man in a bad place, he did what a strong free man would do in order to take care of his son Willie. And that ethic has come on down the line to me, and I have tried over the years to pass it on down to my own children.

George Washington's growth and Great-great-grandmother Jeffries's love and strength are my American stories. I need both of them, as well as my other ancestors and the other patriots, to be who I am and to live the life I have lived. Those were among the thoughts that went through my mind while I was looking toward America from the Atlantic coast of Ghana. The legacies of the American centuries had indeed made me an American. How I will judge the entirety of those legacies and the Virginians who made them will come later.

But it is clear to me now that the founding of the nation was neither so exclusively white nor so deeply flawed by slaveholding that I must feel estranged from it. While my blood is a mixture of many of the strains of the blood of America, I am a black man. I have been shaped by culture, have lived and struggled as a black man, and I look back on both the Revolution and the political founding of the nation as such. I am not alienated by the political founding or by the Revolution; rather, I am profoundly enriched by both. My people did not sit out the tumultuous years of the nation's creation, but made a powerful contribution to it against the heaviest odds. And they did not just endure: they lived and created and passed down strength and power and hope and love as my family inheritance. But I have an American inheritance, too.

In the mid-1980s, I was one of the leaders of the Free South Africa Movement. This was an entirely black-led, multiracial national campaign to reverse the Reagan administration's policy of supporting the apartheid regime in Pretoria. Our fundamental organizational and protest effort was to conduct daily demonstrations during the evening rush hour in front of the South African Embassy on Washington's Massachusetts Avenue, a principal commuting artery to the affluent Maryland suburbs.

Some days we had huge throngs of people, while other days our numbers were very small. One chilly and rainy day when I was the leader, only two other people showed up. We began marching and chanting, "Apartheid must go; Botha must go; Reagan must go!" Famous cynics were writing in the newspapers that our movement was nothing more than a ragtag group of civil rights leftovers who knew nothing of international affairs. We were supposedly just having a temper tantrum because Ronald Reagan had won his second term so handily. When there are only three people marching in the rain, each marcher is individually visible and physically and psychically vulnerable. People in passing cars were giving us quizzical looks or worse, and I was feeling very self-conscious—exposed, I imagined, to disapproval or to ridicule.

My discomfort threatened my capacity to keep up the spirits of our wet and bedraggled little group, and so I tried to fight off my funk.

Why in the world are you feeling self-conscious? I asked myself. All you're doing is exercising your rights as a citizen of the United States. You believe in active citizenship, and you're using your Bill of Rights on behalf of people halfway around the globe who, if they tried to do this in their own capital, would surely be thrown in jail and perhaps even killed.

I immediately felt better and began to act like the leader I was supposed to be. I raised the decibel level of my chants, put more spring in my step, and turned and began to cheer on my compatriots. Although it continued to rain, we kept at it for the hour we had left, and despite the rain and chill, we managed to put on a spirited demonstration. We ended up feeling quite proud that we had held up our end of things though we were drenched and lonely.

We weren't thinking about the founding of the republic that day, or about the Virginia Declaration of Rights, or about George Mason and his colleagues. But considering the limitations on the freedoms of so many across the globe, we were three pretty powerful people. We had an idea of how we wanted to change the world, and we had the freedom to use our spirits, our minds, our bodies, and our bond with one another to strike a small blow for freedom. Our work contributed a bit of the weight that would lead to the collapse of American support for apartheid and ultimately to the rise of South African democracy.

But whether we thought about it or not, hovering over our accomplishment during all the days of our campaign on the streets of Washington and in other cities across the country was, of course, the massive legacy of the founders. While that legacy was forged by members of the founding generation of all colors and from all corners of the thirteen colonies, the role played by four white Virginians, and their contribution to our capacity to be active citizens, were, as I have explained, enormous.

Consider the following sentence, drafted by George Mason approximately 210 years before our march in Washington and issued by the Virginia Convention of 1776 as part of the Virginia Declaration of Rights: "2. That all power is vested in, and consequently derived from the people; that magistrates are their trustees and servants, and at all times amenable to them."

I could not, even on pain of death, have recited those words that day in front of the embassy, but I had them in my bones. I was an American, and I knew that I, as a citizen, was a part of the sovereignty of my nation, that I had rights, and that President Reagan was answerable to the will of the people. It was a knowledge that ran back to my childhood in World War II. Following that "good war" with all the intensity of a child who desperately wanted to be old enough to fly a P-51 against the Nazis, I understood that a major difference between us and our adversaries was that in our country, power flowed up from the people, whereas in the countries we were fighting, it flowed down from the government, which maintained tight control over the citizenry.

Stubborn, impatient, and gouty George Mason drafted the words above and others guaranteeing our citizenship rights in 1776, and then in 1787 he left Philadelphia in a huff because no structure of rights similar to that which he had developed for Virginia had been included in the new federal Constitution. The political maneuvering that he and his Virginia allies, notably Patrick Henry, undertook ultimately forced Madison to promise that he would submit amendments in the First Congress. And true to his word, Madison drew on Mason's work in putting together the country's Bill of Rights, which Congress adopted less than a year before Mason died. This is the first of those amendments: "Congress shall make no law respecting an establishment of religion, or prohibiting the free exercise thereof, or abridging the freedom of speech, or of the press; or the rights of the people peaceably to assemble, and to petition the Government for a redress of grievances."

We were using those rights to the fullest on that wet day on Massachusetts Avenue. We also probably carried in our minds the unexamined assumption that this was the way things would be forever. As we knew from those late-afternoon protests, democracy is precious. And any careful examination of our own history and that of others would have taught us that it is also fragile and perishable.

The founders knew that better than anyone. But they ventured into these uncharted political and emotional waters anyway.

It took great courage, because the unknown and the possibility of chaos can be unsettling to even the sturdiest characters, and positively frightening to those with fainter hearts. But these men bet on their hopes rather than on their fears. They bet that people, when guaranteed freedom, would do what it took to preserve that freedom and would deal with the problems of governing themselves with wisdom and restraint. They drew on their own experience participating in the governance of their colonies, and resisting intrusions into their lives by a government in which they were unable to participate. All of this was grounded in their energetic, even passionate, embrace of Enlightenment ideas about the power of human reason.

The Virginians knew all about unaccountable power, as the words of Mason and Jefferson so eloquently attest. They also knew what happened to people who were entirely subjected to such power—people who had no property, who had not yet entered "into a state of society." The slaves put flesh on their fears. Consequently, Mason and other members of the founding generation were determined to drive protection for the freedoms of the citizens to whom they were bequeathing this new democracy deep into the architecture of the new government, because active citizenship would be central to the success of their revolutionary enterprise.

There was such *good* in the founding, and such glorious promise in the innocent, virginal fields rolling out endlessly toward the far ocean, and such a need for cohesiveness to bind the fragile new nation together, that the simple myths of founding greatness and national innocence were virtually inevitable. As the story of the drafting of the Declaration of Independence indicates, a myth of American decency and innocence was required to justify the violent eruption that ripped apart the old order. Moreover, there was so much evil at the core of American life—emplified by the ethnic cleansing of Native Americans at the expansionist edges of the nation, and by slavery at its cultural and economic heart —that those simple stories of decency and innocence had to be buttressed by the displacement of guilt onto the people who were America's intimate enemies: Native Americans and blacks. Thereby all the founders became simply great, and until recently, the tales told at their plantations about how they lived omitted any mention whatsoever of the slaves upon whom they absolutely depended. Policies toward Native Americans were rarely placed at the center of histories of the early presidents, and Western pulp fiction and, later, pulp movies relentlessly demonized the first Americans. These simplistic myths ballooned in size and power as they hurtled through the generations of a nation in which innocence and guilt became necessary and dominating cultural and political themes.

Abraham Lincoln surely made the most elegant and constructive use of the founding myth when he consecrated the battlefield at Gettysburg. "Four score and seven years ago," the embattled president said, "our fathers brought forth on this continent, a new nation, conceived in Liberty, and dedicated to the proposition that all men are created equal."

This is not an accurate rendering of what "our fathers" did when they ignored the pleas of slaves for shelter under the broad blanket of liberation being fashioned in the Revolution. Nor is it an accurate reading of what they did at the 1787 convention, when they gave slavery constitutional protection, or during the First Congress, where an immigration law was passed restricting citizenship to white people. And it surely isn't an accurate portrayal of what "our fathers," including Lincoln, pursued as Indian policy. But since the truth rarely gets in the way of the desire of nations and individuals to think well of themselves, Lincoln's brilliant use of the myth facilitated the post–Civil War insertion of the promises of the Declaration of Independence into the Constitution as the Thirteenth, Fourteenth, and Fifteenth Amendments.

We have already observed that the truth of the founding was far more complex than we normally imagine. Similarly, the truths of Washington, Mason, Madison, and Jefferson are also far more complicated than the monuments and memories presented to us by the various keepers of the nation's flames have traditionally held. Strangely enough, the remote Washington comes to us most clearly, perhaps because his austere, commanding demeanor defied easy penetration of his soul, and because the texture of his greatness is hard to convey.

The core truth of Washington is that he was an ambitious aristocrat whose character was forged not only under the stars of the wilderness he surveyed as a youth, on horseback, charging across the battlefields of the French and Indian War, but also at the elegant parties held on the estates of his older brother Lawrence and Lawrence's immensely wealthy neighbor Lord Fairfax. The young Washington craved wealth and recognition, and he accepted his inheritance of slavery as natural, one of the necessary and comforting entitlements of his life. Had the Revolution not come along, Washington might well have lived out his life as a fairly unremarkable rich man who voraciously piled wealth upon wealth through aggressive acquisition of land in the West.

But the Revolution did come along, and Washington became *the* indispensable man. Perhaps the war could have been won without him, but it is easy to picture the army melting away during those awful six years between Cambridge and Yorktown, and with it the Revolution, had he not been in command. Maybe the United States would have developed a tradition of civilian rule without him, but he was one leader with a sufficiently firm grip on his ego to return his military commission to the Congress when his duties as a warrior had come to an end. It is possible that the colonies would have sent to the Constitutional Convention their "best characters" even if Washington hadn't agreed to attend, but that hadn't happened in Annapolis eight months earlier. And arguably the convention would have been successful without Washington in the chair. Yet after the ratification of the Constitution, there remained the daunting task of making a real government emerge from the ideas written on that paper, and there was only one person in the new nation whom people trusted to lead that effort. Maybe people could have conceived of a presidency without him, one that would have evolved into a stately, elected office had someone else occupied the chair first, but in the event, Washington was their man.

Isn't it a wonderful coincidence that he was present and out front each step of the way? The man had character, a commanding presence, a brilliant capacity to use subordinates, common sense, a powerful ego and an even more powerful will that kept that ego in check most of the time, and a flat-out, dogged determination to soldier through whatever trials each day brought, no matter how hard the tasks and no matter how long it took. He also knew that he was central to the effort to create a new nation, and he was determined to do his part as effectively as he possibly could. The man had a powerful sense of obligation to his society, and a clear sense of what that obligation required of him.

Those who think Washington elusive, as I once did, and find his greatness hard to define might look to a contemporary figure whose virtues seem very similar to Washington's. In 1990, shortly after he was released from prison, Nelson Mandela toured the United States to raise both consciousness and cash for the African National Congress and the freedom struggle in South Africa. I was fortunate enough to be asked by his host, the entertainer Harry Belafonte, to coordinate that trip, so I had the opportunity to be with Mandela for ten days as he traveled across America.

In every city he visited, from Boston to Oakland, he was showered with the hysterical love and enthusiasm that sports fans reserve for a team that has just won a world championship. Everyone from President George H. W. Bush to homeless people wanted to look at him, to cheer him, to touch him. Mandela calmly absorbed all of this without any apparent change in his view of himself. Nevertheless, he was acutely aware of the extent of America's affection for him and for what he symbolized, and he utilized that aspect of his life on the tour as a tool for the job he had come to do. He got up every morning and went to work, using himself and the meaning that people attached to him as instruments in the struggle to overthrow apartheid and create a democracy in South Africa. He was not without ego, but he understood that the cause to which he was devoted was larger than himself. He worked inside that cause and made it stronger.

Like Washington, Mandela led through character, not through eloquence; like him, he had a strong ego on which he kept a firm grip. Mandela's self-reliance and rock-hard integrity were likewise formed in adversity, outside the normal fountains of privilege that so often bear people up to positions of critical prominence and power. Like Washington, Mandela was able to curb his normal human need for self-aggrandizement in order to devote himself to a larger cause. And like Washington, Mandela, in choosing to subordinate his ego to serve his country, earned immortality.

When Washington died, at the close of the century in December 1799, many people wondered whether the country would dissolve with him. But the foundation of stability that he and his colleagues had put in place with such effort and care precluded that possibility.

George Mason shared Washington's covetous interest in Western land. In the peacetime years, the surveyor and the real estate lawyer had consulted at length about their common interests. It was natural, then, for Washington, during the "Real American Revolution," to turn time after time to his old neighbor for advice and assistance. Seven years older and born into a more comfortable family position than Washington, Mason was a far more settled burgher than his restless, on-the-make colleague, who was his father's third son, by his second wife. Mason, in contrast, was his father's firstborn son. He, too, was a haughty aristocrat, more intellectual than his neighbor but also testier and more firmly anchored to his family and his land. Mason's political contributions were limited not only by his intolerance of the human frailties of the common run of legislators, but also by his family responsibilities, particularly after his wife died, leaving him to raise their children alone. Perhaps it was his devotion to family—the acute sense of being Colonel George Mason IV, with George Mason V and several other children growing up under his wing—that convinced Mason to include his slaves in his will like furniture or cattle, in spite of his elegant and oft-expressed disdain for slavery.

Despite his impatience with legislative work, his ill health, and his desire to be at home with his family, Mason still made a significant contribution to the founding. Most important here was his devotion to the rights of citizens against the weight and authority of government. The supreme display of his flinty integrity came when he successfully insisted that those rights be enshrined in the fundamental legal framework of the United States.

The founder most obsessed with ensuring that the country would "long endure," however, was Madison. Unlike Mason, in pursuit of that goal he made it his business to get along with other legislators and to be present when and where great events were occurring. His career demonstrates that he was devoted to rights and to the aura of freedom, but his real passion turned out to be the stability and the strength of the nation that he and his colleagues were establishing. People often ask why I like James Madison so, bookish and boring as he seems to have been. I liken him to Cal Ripken, whose record for consecutive major-league baseball games played may never be broken, and who showed up for work every day completely prepared and then delivered day in and day out for as long as he was able to do that work.

Madison was brilliant, a consummate analyst and strategist, a fine writer, and one of the most exceptional legislators this country has ever known. In addition to being a bear for work, he was utterly self-possessed. He could thus sit through the most arduous legislative proceedings with his mind at work and his ego in check. In addition to contributing to the creation of the Constitution and its ratification, he was a mainstay of Washington's first term, of Jefferson's legislative work and spirit, and of the First Congress and the first political party. He was a good part of the glue that kept the new contraption from flying apart in its early stages, as well as the principal author of the machinery that kept it running over the long haul.

A study of his observations about freeing his slave Billey suggests that Madison's innate sensibility about slavery was closer to that of the Quaker abolitionists than was the thinking of any of the other three members of this Virginia quartet. And yet he did not lift a finger in the Constitutional Convention to prohibit the continuance of the international slave trade, to block the bloating of the slaveocracy's legislative power by counting only 60 percent of the slaves as its constituents, or to forestall the inclusion of a fugitive-slave clause in the document. The reason for his reticence in this area was that his passion to achieve a governmental design that would serve the urgent needs of the nation as he perceived them took primacy over all other values; adjustments could be made later, he believed. But he never managed to mount an effective campaign to "adjust" slavery out of American life. Instead he dithered, and at the end of his own life he could only fret impotently about the horrors of the practice and the great psychic burdens it placed on white women.

Madison was quite clear-eyed about the future. The founders were entitled to conclude that, by defeating the military behemoth over the ocean to the east and fashioning a new government based on a novel faith in the people and an innovative way of distributing national power, they had created something new in the world. They then turned their backs on the old world to the east and faced America's future where it lay, over the mountains to the west. Madison and Jefferson shared a powerful optimism about that western future, one that may well have been driven into their psyches by their family histories. Madison's great-grandfather James Taylor II had been one of the "Knights of the Golden Horseshoe" who had accompanied Governor Alexander Spotswood on an exploration of the Virginia Piedmont in 1716. Jefferson's father, Peter, was a surveyor and frontiersman whose energies were centered on efforts to explore and tame "the West." Thomas Jefferson built his life on family land in what was then the western reach of Virginia. Montpelier, Madison's home, was near Monticello, and from his front veranda Madison could look west and enjoy a dramatic and beautiful view of the Blue Ridge Mountains.

With the new so close at hand and the old so recently defeated, it is no wonder that these men and others like them were hopeful about the good future that awaited America on the other side of the Shenandoah. Jefferson, for his part, held tightly to the conviction that Europe and especially the circle around the British Crown and council were entirely corrupt; in his mind, America should be *really* new—not a vast land strewn with fetid cities, but an agrarian nation peopled by virtuous and energetic yeoman farmers. Madison even published an essay in 1791 in which he argued that the Malthusian population dilemma could be solved by European immigration and settlement in the West, where moral improvement could be achieved far away from sinful urban cesspools. The essay appeared less than a year after Congress enacted a whites-only immigration law. Around this same time, the effort to get Native Americans out of the way and plans to colonize blacks in Africa were both picking up steam.

There were only two problems with the dreamy vision that Madison and Jefferson shared. First, as George Mason had noted a few decades earlier, human beings didn't change their nature just because they crossed the Atlantic Ocean; and second, a pure white America had never existed and never would. Yet the myth about the future was grafted onto the earlier mythological telling of the story of the Great White Revolution carried out by Great White Men. These myths tied American virtue to American whiteness, and with each passing generation the whole simplistic amalgam became embedded in our culture as historical memory. For many it was a compelling story of American splendor fording streams and rivers, crossing prairies and climbing mountains bravely, ceaselessly, and inevitably into an ever-brighter future. It was a gratifying notion, but in many respects it was just not true.

It worked, of course, as it had in colonial Virginia, for the privileged, the powerful, the nimble and energetic, the ruthless and the lucky. For those upon whom fortune did not smile so warmly, the American mythology was a far more complicated proposition. The stories promised too much, turning the pursuit of happiness into a psychic trail of torture for the many whites who were locked out of the structures of America's opportunity. If happiness was virtually guaranteed to whites in a land where the losers were to be nonstandard humans with darker skins, how could a poor white man explain his lifelong failures to himself? And how could successful and sensitive whites incorporate into their consciousness the glaring exceptions to the American story line? Supporting myths and "memories" about racial superiority and contempt for otherness, laced with tales of white nobility in contacts with lesser races, were developed to smooth out incongruities and sown throughout both scholarly works and popular culture. Generations of blacks and Native Americans, cast as despoilers of an otherwise idyllic white paradise, groaned beneath the weight of the multiple brutalities and constrictions these complex but simple-minded cultural neuroses imposed upon them.

Perhaps no other early American embodied in his life and work a more complete refutation of the simplistic and exclusionary story of America's origins and growth than Thomas Jefferson. He was a great but deeply flawed human being who depended more heavily on the blacks around him than any of the other founders. He came down to us deep into the twentieth century with the greatness etched out in bold, bright strokes and the frailties airbrushed into the black holes of history. The founding legacy contains a powerful *aura* of freedom that is much broader in scope and deeper in the culture than the actual concepts embedded in the law. The opening phrases of Lincoln's address at Gettysburg, for example, are drawn not just from the Bill of Rights but from a sense that the very idea of America is steeped in the dedication to human freedom. Over the centuries, Americans have settled on Thomas Jefferson as the principal progenitor of the generous spirit of American freedom. It is a judgment that I myself found hard to dispute that day when I stood inside the Jefferson Memorial and tried to puzzle from the founder's sculpted likeness and his words carved into marble what furies must have clashed inside his soul. He was a dizzying mixture of searing brilliance and infuriating self-indulgence, of idealism and base racism, of soaring patriotism and myopic self-involvement. He was America writ small.

It is odd that Jefferson, who started out as a real estate lawyer, would be best remembered as a romantic philosopher with a poetic touch. The transformation was made possible by the wealth in slaves he acquired on the death of his father-in-law, which gave him the leisure to study, to reflect, and to write. He became the bard of freedom largely because powerful strands of Enlighten-

ment thought and Whiggish resentment struck deep and respon-
sive chords in his soul. He, more than any other member of the
founding generation, was able to capture the zeitgeist of those
movements and to give them eloquent voice. He didn't have to be
original; it was the elegance of his prose, fueled by his passion, that
moved human spirits and made him immortal.

Jefferson's passions led him to excess as well as brilliance. His
assertion that the "tree of liberty needs to be nourished by blood
every generation or so" sounds sophomoric to twenty-first-cen-
tury ears. His argument in "Rights of British North America"
that the original colonials had established themselves with no help
from England was a transparent stretch of the truth, flung down to
support his argument that Parliament had no authority to legislate
for the colonies; and his charge that the slave trade was the chief
problem with slavery and that it was entirely the fault of King
George made him look foolish.

Yet a powerful argument could also be made that with a little
editing help from his colleagues in the Second Continental Congress, Jefferson, in polishing Mason's words about the natural
rights of humankind, coauthored the most significant sentence in
American history. None of the founders bore a greater share of responsibility for freedom of religion than Jefferson. And he believed that the new nation that he had done so much to help create
provided greater nurturing and protection for the human spirit
than any previous regime on earth.

But Jefferson also spent a lot of time nurturing and protecting
himself, sometimes to the great detriment of those around him.
His passivity during the Revolutionary War—even during his
term as governor of Virginia—seems most curious. Much later,
having urged President Washington to hang on for a second term
to hold the nation together, Jefferson left the cabinet and then
took shots at the old soldier, often sheltered behind someone else's
pen. After remaining silent for years on the issue of freedom for
blacks, he indulged his personal tastes, his intellectual interests,
and his hobbies so promiscuously that his debts overwhelmed
him. He was thus forced to sell off some of his slaves to reconcile

accounts, leaving most of the rest to be scattered at his death on the winds of his creditors' whims. He included a vile racist screed in his *Notes on the State of Virginia* and in his old age, as a leading sage of the nation, turned aside the pleas of his earnest and idealistic young friend Edward Coles, who begged him to take some dramatic step against slavery or at least denounce it forcefully. He maintained until his death that he wished there was some way for blacks to be exported so that the slavery he so detested could be eradicated; yet he found it impossible to live a slaveless life. From his earliest memory of being carried on a pillow by one slave to the day he was lowered into the earth in a coffin made by another, Thomas Jefferson led a life cushioned by the subjugation of others.

On the issue of Sally Hemings, Jefferson turns out to have been a serious hypocrite. He wrote vigorous denunciations of miscegenation even as it was clearly occurring with some regularity at Monticello. Either he was participating in it himself, as the DNA evidence seems to suggest, or, as the white Jefferson family told it, one of his nephews fathered Ms. Hemings's children (a claim refuted by the DNA evidence). In any event, the patriarch of the plantation had it in his power to stop the exploitation of Sally Hemings, and he did not choose to do so. To describe Jefferson as purely great is to do an enormous disservice to the humanity of this profoundly human man, and to undervalue the many occasions on which he rose above the ordinary messiness of his spirit to leave great gifts to posterity.

Whites who confronted their culture and opposed slavery and racial oppression add a further dimension to the picture. As noted above, Edward Coles, a young protégé of both Jefferson and Madison, gave those two great Virginians a last chance, late in their lives, to get on the right side of history on the issue of slavery. Both declined, so Coles decided to act on his own. He moved to Illinois, where he educated and freed his own slaves and was ultimately elected governor. In Pennsylvania there was Anthony Benezet, whom the scholar Maurice Jackson has called "America's finest eighteenth-century antislavery advocate." While Benezet never owned slaves himself, he devoted his life to improving the lot of blacks in general by advocating the abolition of slavery, and to helping them individually by teaching slaves in the African Free School. One of his students was Absalom Jones. Seeing through the Virginia fathers' claim that slavery was entirely the fault of the despotic London promoters of the international slave trade, Benezet laid a substantial share of the blame where it belonged: on the shoulders of those Americans who built their lives on the fruits of that trade. He fiercely opposed any suggestion that blacks were inferior to whites.

Coles and Benezet confound the simplistic thinking that many blacks fall into, which holds that virtually all whites of the founding generation both North and South were complicit in the slave trade, and that most of them benefitted from it. These two men were secular saints who, despite the fierce demands of their culture to the contrary, followed their consciences and paid whatever price was required. The four founders from Virginia left massive legacies to the nation, but they were unable to figure out how to shake off the shackles of privilege. Thus, while Washington freed his slaves, thereby sending a powerful message of disapproval of slavery down through the generations and complicating his own legacy, he did not live a moment of his life without the buffer that slavery provided.

The founders didn't think of themselves, one another, or their generation as secular saints. The way they designed our government is a clear demonstration of their cast of mind. They saw human weakness all around them, as Mason's fulminations about the shortcomings of Virginia legislators attest. These founders understood that they had been shaped, like all of us, by inherited culture. Under the tutelage of their fathers, Virginia youngsters born into the aristocracy in the early to mid–eighteenth century were groomed from birth to accept the privileges they had inherited. In the end this inheritance would engulf them. Nothing illuminates the problem better than Patrick Henry's reaction to an antislavery book sent to him by Benezet: "Every thinking honest man rejects it [slavery] in Speculation, how few in practice? Would any one believe that I am Master of slaves of my own purchase? I am drawn along by ye general Inconvenience of living without them; I will not, I cannot justify it."

Privilege is addictive. The most natural thing in the world is for each human being to view the privilege he enjoys as, well, the most natural thing in the world.

I remember a privilege of my own. The Korean War broke out at the end of my freshman year in college. The United States still had the draft, and I was very pleased to be classified 2-S. People in that category enjoyed a student deferment as long as they stayed in college and pursued a degree. That policy seemed reasonable to me and to every other college student I knew. The war would be a frequent topic of our bull sessions in Ann Arbor over the ensuing three years, and I remember *no one's* questioning our privileged status; we all agreed that the notion of not risking the lives of the "best brains in the country" was both wise and just. It was only when I learned of the war death of an able contemporary who couldn't afford college that doubt began to nibble at my certitude about the justice of my own good fortune.

When I think of my relative wealth as compared to poor people in my own country and in the developing world, and how little help I offer, I wonder how *I* would survive history's most intense scrutiny. I wonder the same thing as I hum along alone in my powerful European sedan, commuting between work and home on a route just parallel to a public transportation system. One might argue that slavery was worse. Consuming comfortably while millions of malnourished and therefore doomed children across the globe suffer in poverty, or helping to make the planet uninhabitable—how do these things stack up against slavery? I can't be sure, but I do know that though these are among the greatest moral challenges of my time, I am addicted, like the founding fathers, to my privileges and their convenience.

Nevertheless, I do judge the slave-owning founders harshly, and I grind my teeth for my ancestors who suffered during the Middle Passage and under the lash. But I do so as a person who tries to accept the weight of his own moral flaws on his soul, one who wants, at least, to be a good person. The founding slave owners were more than good men; they were great men. But when myth presents them as secular saints, and when an attempt is made to whitewash their ownership of slaves and the deep legacy of racism that they helped to institutionalize, the impulse to pull them and the works of their whole generation off their pedestals becomes exceedingly strong.

There has been no more powerful and elegant symbolic challenge to the legacy of the founders than the gauntlet thrown down by Frederick Douglass on July 4, 1852, against the "Spirit of '76," shrouded as it was in the mythology of national idealism, innocence, and virtue. He took his American experience as a slave and pounded it on the words of the Declaration of Independence and the moral pretensions of Americans. Speaking in Rochester, New York, the abolitionist and self-freed former slave said this about America:

> What to the American slave is your Fourth of July? I answer, a day that reveals to him more than all other days of the year, the gross injustice and cruelty to which he is the constant victim. To him your celebration is a sham; your boasted liberty an unholy license; your national greatness, swelling vanity; your sounds of rejoicing are empty and heartless; your denunciations of tyrants, brass-fronted impudence; your shouts of liberty and equality, hollow mockery; your prayers and hymns, your sermons and thanksgivings, with all your religious parade and solemnity, are to him mere bombast, fraud, deception, impiety, and hypocrisy—a thin veil to cover up crimes that would disgrace a nation of savages. There is not a nation of the earth guilty of practices more shocking and bloody than are the people of the United States at this very hour.

Douglass would continue to struggle for justice until the end of his life. He was a giant in the great American tradition, using the idealistic legacy of the founders to enrich democracy as it is actually lived in the land, and in so doing, employing another of the great legacies of the founding: active citizenship.

It is that inheritance of democratic agency that enabled the young republic to survive and, more important, to evolve. The point is made in a story told about Benjamin Franklin. After participating in the secret deliberations during which the Constitution was drafted, Franklin is said to have encountered an inquisitive woman in Philadelphia and to have had the following exchange with her:

"What have you made for us, Dr. Franklin?"

"A republic, madam, if you can keep it."

If you can keep it. Franklin understood that democracy was not forever assured to the United States, and that active citizenship would be required to keep and enhance it. The contentious debates over the terms of the Constitution had confirmed what the founders already knew, that democracy was hard work, and they left us a heroic example of how to *do* that work. The rights-conscious political system embedded in a stable governmental structure initially made it possible for good white men to be political, and on the issues of race, good men and women have subsequently built upon that legacy, carving out a story that should glitter in memory for as long as records of human achievements endure. It is the as-yet-unfinished story of the abolition of chattel slavery in America and the rise of blacks out of that muck and misery, and of whites' gradual abandonment of the chains of sinful racial privilege and constricted human understanding, and of the extension of freedom and opportunities to women, gays and lesbians, and all other minority groups in the country. It is the story that I reflect upon each Fourth of July, because the Declaration of Independence, for all the ambiguity around it, constitutes the Big Bang in the physics of freedom and equality in America.

Douglass's words were absolutely appropriate when he spoke them. But eleven years later at Gettysburg, under the pressure of a horribly bloody war, Abraham Lincoln would give his own meaning to the text of the Declaration of Independence. Still later, after the North won the war, Lincoln's revisions would be embedded in the Constitution as the Thirteenth, Fourteenth, and Fifteenth Amendments. In the thirteen decades since, America has evolved and changed, pushed by the ideals planted in our culture by the founders and by the efforts of determined and courageous citizens committed to reshaping the nation according to those ideals. The frontiers of freedom in the United States have been so greatly enlarged that neither the Frederick Douglass of 1852 nor the Abraham Lincoln of 1863 would now recognize the nation in which the struggles of his lifetime were fought. Neither would it look familiar to my great-great-grandmother ———— Jeffries, and even my father, who died in 1941, would be amazed at the America of 2000 and the opportunities enjoyed by his son and by the grandchildren he did not live to meet.

My own participation in many of the struggles that have created that change has left me feeling fulfilled about the work of my life. But I am far from content. Cruel injustice abounds in this society, and far, far too much racism persists both in the formulation of public policy and in such ordinary places as personnel departments, country-club locker rooms, and bankers' offices, where private decisions can be pivotal in determining not only individual fates but the whole texture of community life. Virulent anti-black feelings still proliferate in America, and not just in the hearts of people who kill out of hatred or join white supremacist organizations. There are "decent" Americans who not only are unmoved by the fact that 40 percent of black children are living in poverty, but use that fact to buttress their own convictions about black inferiority. There are Americans who think it reasonable that blacks should constitute 49 percent of America's bulging prison population and 35 percent of those who have been executed since that punishment was revived fourteen years ago. And there are those who ignore persistent disparities between black and white health, income, wealth, educational attainment, and employment. These same people regularly exert enormous efforts to destroy the fragile programs put into place in the sixties and seventies to compensate for the deep injuries done to blacks over the three and a half centuries of their legally sanctioned subordination. As a result of the brilliant rhetorical propaganda that has accompanied the assault on such programs, quiet racism has again become a potent factor in American life; its principal victims, as usual, are the black poor.

My recurring nightmare in recent years has been that there will be such a significant separation of the black upper and middle classes from poor blacks that when America declares total victory over antiblack racism, substantial numbers of well-off blacks and members of other minorities will be complicit in the deceit. We will then have a society much like that found in Brazil. We could tell ourselves that we have a "racial democracy" here, and overlook the fact that the only thing the blacks at the bottom have in abundance is misery, made permanent by their virtually complete lack of access to the national opportunity structure. We will have put the finishing touches on our national scapegoat: an untouchable, impoverished caste of permanent mudsills, filling a role not at all unlike the one John Smith had in mind for Native Americans almost four centuries ago.

It may seem strange, given such ruminations, that I consider myself to be enthusiastically patriotic, but here I am, raised and aged in the midst of the American reality. To be human is to live with moral complexity and existential ambiguity. I don't need for this nation to be perfect in order for me to love it; I love it because it is home, and because all of the touchstones of my life are here. More than anything, though, I suppose I love the opportunity this nation affords me to engage in struggles for decency. That, in my view, is the greatest legacy of the founders. The governmental system, wrapped in the aura of freedom and limited by a devotion to rights, has created the field on which so many of us of different races, genders, and sexual orientations have been able to grow into full and potent citizens. Whereas some people view America primarily as a place of economic opportunity, I see it as having afforded me the chance to make something of myself by exerting relentless energy in the effort to hold up my end.

When I am so engaged, I think of an English contemporary of the Virginia founders, Edmund Burke. Burke, who accepted life as humans lived it, once observed, "The only thing necessary for evil to prevail is for good men to remain silent." He did not believe that humans were perfectible, or that the civilizing limits we try to place on ourselves could tame all human appetites all the time. Principles of decency have to be reinforced on a daily basis, and the creation of models of honorable conduct has to be a permanent enterprise. Evil is a basic element of nature: the seeds are in all of us. Good has to be manufactured and pushed energetically into public affairs. It is willed into the world by human effort. The system bequeathed by the founders protects people as they try to rally themselves and like-minded others to undertake tasks that they believe will contribute to the public good. It also leaves to the general will of the people the ultimate judgment about which "good" will prevail.

In my view, we have created much good. There is clearly much more to be done, and there always will be. But it is deeply American to aspire to make things better. Only a growling surliness about how bad things are, especially for me and mine (whoever a particular "me" or "we" may be), is toxic in our political culture. I often tell my students that the opportunity to engage in active citizenship is the greatest gift of their country. I tell my black students that they are far more than the sum of their pain and their grievances, my white students that they are more than the sum of their privileges and their resentments. And finally, I tell them all that it is a lie that "there's nothing certain but death and taxes." Nothing is certain but death, taxes, and *change*. We can either effect the change that is sure to come or stand immobile and be swept away by the change that others have shaped. Consequently, I try to pound into my students' minds the idea that democracy is precious and fragile and that its survival can be guaranteed down through the generations only by a citizenry that is well informed, alert, and active. I tell them about Edmund Burke and assure them that they, too, can create good. In contemplating the political, demographic, and cultural issues we will face in the next half century or so, we would do well to remember the wishes Washington expressed for us in his "last Circular" to the states as commander in chief of the Continental Army, issued in 1783. His final observation about what he thought was essential to the new nation called for "the prevalence of that pacific and friendly disposition among the people of the United States which will induce them to forget their local prejudices and policies, to make those mutual concessions which are requisite to the general prosperity, and in some instances, to sacrifice their individual advantages to the interest of the community."

We Americans have a wonderful political legacy that is, in part, the work of people who owned people very much like me. It is possible that some of those they owned were among my ancestors. The lives of these founders and their characters were indelibly stained by that fact, though the heinousness of the crime may be relieved a bit by the fact that they were born into an existence anchored in slavery. It might reasonably be asked why I keep returning to the point that these four men were inheritors of a slave society and were shaped from birth by its culture. The answer is that I, like many others who share my views, feel that culture should be a major factor in informing contemporary public policies regarding poor Americans. That is, I deeply believe that we need to take into account the damage done by the deprivations and humiliations we have inflicted over the generations on poor people, limiting their capacity to cope with our society. And I believe that we need to craft compensatory programs to open paths of opportunity for them. But surely I cannot on the one hand argue that cultural forces can injure people for whom I have ethnic empathy, and on the other refuse to recognize and make allowances for just such cultural injuries in the lives of the founders. To paraphrase the wonderful truism that Walt Kelly put into Pogo's mouth: I have met the founders, and they are us.

I say *us* as a deeply committed American. One famous African American has been quoted recently as saying, "At no time have I ever felt like an American." Well, *I* have—all my life. When I was a child rooting for Jesse Owens and Joe Louis, I was an American kid rooting for genuine American heroes. When I was twelve and dreamed of flying a P-51 Mustang against the Luftwaffe, I was a fantasy American warrior. And when the white adolescents in Grand Rapids spat on my bike seat and threw stones and apple cores at me, I was having a deeply American experience.

Those kids were attempting to define me as something other

than and smaller than American: a Nigger. That was not their privilege. Nor was it the privilege of the odd white teacher or two who suggested that my mind was limited and my aspirations should be as well. Down through the decades, there were others who tried to make my blackness constricting. But they didn't have the privilege, either.

The privilege of defining me rests with my African ancestors, who had the fortitude to survive the Middle Passage and the "seasoning" meted out by their new American jailers. It rests with those Enlightenment philosophers who inserted the idea of human equality into the ideology of the West—and that would surely include the founders of America, notably including Thomas Jefferson, that quintessential man of ambiguity. It rests with Abraham Lincoln, who redefined the meaning of the founding, and with the Radical Republicans who put those ideas into the Constitution in the Thirteenth, Fourteenth, and Fifteenth Amendments. It rests with Crispus Attucks and all the other blacks who fought in the Revolution and in every American war after that. It rests with the slaves whose stolen lives built so much of the strength and wealth of this country. It rests with the abolitionists both white and black who would not let their idea die. It rests with every American of whatever color or political persuasion who carried the fight down to my generation so that my mentors, colleagues, and friends could carry it on. And of course, it rests with my grandparents and my parents.

But, most of all, the privilege of defining me rests with my slave ancestors, most prominently, Mound and ———— Jeffries and Emma and Asberry Wilkins. To cede the definition of what an American is or what I am to pigment patriots who attach Confederate flags to the grilles of the tractors pulling their huge highway rigs and who wear American-flag tattoos, or to bigoted legislators who take from the poor to give to the rich, is to give up the entire lives of my slave ancestors and all of the other decent people who contributed to the fight for American justice.

That is not my privilege.

I accept the possibility that my understanding of America may be skewed by the extraordinary advances made in my lifetime, which is, after all, only a snippet in the long sweep of almost four hundred years from the Jamestown landing down to our globalized, cyberspace era. I have seen and participated in a remarkable enlargement of American opportunity and justice over the course of my life. From the one-room segregated schoolhouse in Missouri where I started school, through a lifelong apprenticeship and friendship with Thurgood Marshall and a rich variety of struggles for justice, I have had the great fortune to see and participate in an astonishing American effort to adjust life as it is lived to the ideals proclaimed by the founders. While the transformation is far from complete, the change has nevertheless been so dramatic that my belief in American possibilities remains profound. It could be argued that I have lived through an aberrant period in American history, and therefore my modest optimism is misplaced. Perhaps, but I still believe in the power of citizen action harnessed to our founding ideals to improve American life and even to transform some American hearts. I have seen the process work.

But what I have seen surely doesn't mean that I am free to accept a separate peace and turn my back on the most vulnerable people in the country. This includes, most notably, the poorest blacks and the poorest Native Americans and Latinos, who, because of their beaten condition, often seem unattractive and frightening to most Americans, even me sometimes. But instead of recoiling from them in rage and fear, we should allow our intense reaction to their near (or in some cases total) defeat to motivate us to change our culture so that the cascade of destruction from generation to generation may be slowed and finally halted.

Occasionally, while internalizing that destruction and its attendant human waste and pain, I have made speeches that reeked of hopelessness. People who have heard me in that mood sometimes ask how I manage to keep going. My answer is that my ancestors lift me up when I am low. Some of them never drew a free breath, and others drew very few of them. I try to live as if I am going to have to meet them someday and answer the question "Boy, how did you use your freedom?" The only conceivable an-

swer is that I have tried to live up to the standards of honor and fortitude that they set for me.

And so with Edmund Burke's realism in my mind, with the
physics of freedom bequeathed by the founders in my heart, and
with my slave ancestors in my soul, I just keep on being an active
American reveling in the struggle that is both my life and, after my
ancestors, my most precious American legacy.

NOTES

1. Tainted Origins

11 *"a man who spends most of his time in retirement"*: Robert A. Rutland, ed., *The Papers of George Mason,* vol. 1, *1748–1778* (Chapel Hill: University of North Carolina Press, 1970), 65.

13 *"One day, when all our people were gone"*: "The Life of Gustavus Vassa," in Henry Louis Gates, Jr., ed., *The Classic Slave Narratives* (New York: Mentor Books/New American Library, 1987), 25.

16 *white stood for purity and beauty, and black for evil and filth:* Winthrop Jordan, *The White Man's Burden: Historical Origins of Racism in the United States* (London: Oxford University Press, 1974), 6, 14.

16 *Thus, when the English began to collide with people unlike themselves:* For my understanding throughout this text of life in Colonial Virginia, I am deeply indebted to Edmund S. Morgan, particularly for the broad, rich analysis set out in his *American Slavery, American Freedom: The Ordeal of Colonial Virginia* (New York: W. W. Norton & Co., 1975).

17 *"The Epithets of Parent & Child":* Rutland, *The Papers of George Mason,* 1:65.

20 *Practical lessons in . . . privileges:* John Ferling, *Setting the World Ablaze: Washington, Adams, Jefferson and the American Revolution* (London: Oxford University Press, 2000), 5.

23 *"by 1705 Virginia had rationalized . . . its exclusion of blacks":* A. Leon Higgenbotham, Jr., *In the Matter of Color: Race and the American Legal Process: The Colonial Period* (London: Oxford University Press, 1978), 58.

23 *some owners found it expedient to "season" newly imported Africans:* Peter Kolchin, *American Slavery: 1619–1877* (New York: Hill and Wang, 1993), 57.

25 *"Like one of the patriarchs of old":* William Byrd II to Charles, earl of Orrey, July 5, 1726, quoted in Rhys, Isaac, *The Transformation of Virginia: 1740–1790* (New York: W. W. Norton & Co., 1988), 39.

26   *"that all men are by nature equally free and independent":* Quoted in Robert
      Allen Rutland, *George Mason: Reluctant Statesman* (Williamsburg, Va.:
      Colonial Williamsburg, 1961), 53.

28   *Henry Ireton . . . held that the right to vote rested on a "permanent fixed interest
      in the Kingdom":* Aspen Institute, *The Executive Seminar: The Aspen Insti-
      tute Readings, Vol. 2* (Aspen, Colo.: Aspen Institute, 1997), 55.

28   *"I think that the poorest he that is in England hath a life to live, as the greatest
      he":* Ibid., 59.

29   *The writings of many seventeenth- and early-eighteenth-century theorists in
      England and Scotland . . . were used as fuel:* Bernard Baylin, *The Ideological
      Origins of the American Revolution* (Cambridge, Mass.: Belknap/Harvard,
      1992), 36.

31   *"It was very much the practice with Gentlemen of landed and Slave Estates":*
      Unpublished reflections of George Mason's son John, displayed at Guns-
      ton Hall, Lorton, Virginia.

2. Bright Promises, Shadows of Sin

38   *"At a time when our lordly Masters in Great Britain will be satisfied with noth-
      ing less than deprication [sic] of American freedom":* Quoted in Douglas
      Southall Freeman, *Washington,* one-volume abridgement, by Richard
      Harwell, of Freeman's seven-volume biography (New York: Collier
      Books/Macmillan, 1968), 174.

39   *Mason's draft . . . expressing the desire that " 'an entire stop' could be put to the
      'wicked cruel and unnatural' slave trade":* Robert Allen Rutland, *George
      Mason: Reluctant Statesman* (Williamsburg, Va.: Colonial Williamsburg,
      1961), 39.

39   *"It is our greatest wish . . . to continue our connection with and dependence upon
      the British government; but":* Quoted in Freeman, *Washington,* 203.

40   *"These are our grievances":* Quoted in Willard Sterne Randall, *Thomas
      Jefferson: A Life* (New York: Harper Perennial, 1994), 213.

42   *"The possibility of a slave rebellion was never far out of white consciousness":*
      Robert Middelkauff, *The Glorious Cause: The American Revolution,
      1763–1789* (New York: Oxford University Press, 1982), 316.

42   *"Unhappy it is . . . to reflect that a brother's sword has been sheathed in a broth-
      er's breast":* Quoted in Freeman, *Washington,* 217.

42   *"we will use every means . . . to prevent our becoming . . . slaves":* Quoted
      ibid., 203.

44   *Dunmore was an "Arch Traitor":* Fritz Hirschfeld, *George Washington and Slavery* (Columbia, Mo.: University of Missouri Press, 1997), 143.

45   *"the most important [step] that ever was taken in America":* Quoted in John Ferling, *Setting the World Ablaze: Washington, Adams, Jefferson and the American Revolution* (London: Oxford University Press, 2000), 131.

45   *"A wealthy planter, often aloof from colonial politics":* Ralph Ketcham, *James Madison* (Charlottesville, Va.: University Press of Virginia, 1990), 71.

46   *John Adams would later recall that he had prevailed upon Jefferson to prepare the first draft because he was a Virginian and wrote brilliantly:* Pauline Maier, *American Scripture: Making the Declaration of Independence* (New York: Alfred A. Knopf, 1997), 99.

46   *"Throughout the remainder of his long career Jefferson never again experienced a challenge better suited to call forth his best creative energies"* Joseph Ellis, *American Sphinx: The Character of Thomas Jefferson* (New York: Alfred A. Knopf, 1997), 50.

47   *"He has waged cruel war against human nature itself":* Maier, *American Scripture,* 239.

48   *"Ironically it was slavery that suddenly made Thomas Jefferson free of his tedious, unremunerative law practice":* Randall, *Thomas Jefferson,* 180.

49   *"the emotional climax of his case against the King":* Maier, *American Scripture,* 121.

50   *blacks "formed no part of the people who framed and adopted this declaration":* Chief Justice Roger Taney, *Dred Scott v. Sanford,* Howard 393 (1857).

3. The Wages of Privilege

53   *"all men are equally entitled to the free exercise of religion, according to the dictates of conscience":* Quoted in Ralph Ketcham, *James Madison* (Charlottesville, Va.: University Press of Virginia, 1990), 71.

53   *the authority of the new nation was leaking from its principal source to thirteen different seats:* Douglas Southall Freeman, *Washington* (New York: Collier Books/Macmillan, 1968), 528.

54   *He asked his friend Jefferson . . . to scour the bookstalls of Paris:* R. W. conversation with guide at Montpelier, August 13, 1997.

54   *Madison recorded "the facts and lessons about . . . confederacies in a booklet of forty-one pocket-sized pages":* Ketcham, *James Madison,* 184.

54   *In August 1786, he left Montpelier . . . to attend a meeting . . . to "examine the trade of the states":* Ibid., 185.

55   *In 1787 Jefferson noted that Madison had "acquired a habit of self-possession, which placed at ready command the rich resources of his luminous and discriminating mind"*: Ibid., 189.

56   *Daniel Shays and his followers—described as "desperate and unprincipled men"*: Quoted in Freeman, *Washington*, 534.

57   *Early on [Mason] declared that he was "heartily tired of the etiquette and nonsense so fashionable in [Philadelphia]"*: Robert Allen Rutland, *George Mason: Reluctant Statesman* (Williamsburg, Va.: Colonial Williamsburg, 1961), 85.

58   *"History will never be able to assess the extent of the contribution Washington made through such personal contacts"*: James Thomas Flexner, *Washington: The Indispensable Man* (1969; reprint, Boston: Back Bay Books, 1994), 207.

59   *"[I] chose a seat in front of the president member . . . [a] favorable position for hearing all that passed"*: Quoted in Ketcham, *James Madison*, 195.

59   *Mason's passion for constitutions of the "democratic kind"*: Ibid., 200.

62   *Luther Martin . . . summed up the dilemma by damning the slave trade as inconsistent with the revolutionary theories of freedom based on natural law*: Quoted in Robert Middelkauff, *The Glorious Cause: The American Revolution, 1763–1789* (New York: Oxford University Press, 1982), 646.

62   *"Religion and humanity have nothing to do with this question"*: Quoted in Richard Kluger, *Simple Justice* (New York: Vintage Books, 1977), 33.

62   *"The present question concerns not the importing states alone but the whole Union"*: Ibid., 34.

63   *"The Migration or Importation of such Persons as any of the States now existing shall think proper to admit, shall not be prohibited by the Congress prior to the Year one thousand eight hundred and eight"*: Constitution of the United States, Article I, Section 9 [1].

63   *"No Person held to Service or Labour in one State"*: Ibid., Article IV, Section 2 [3].

64   *Mason left for home . . . "in an exceeding ill humour"*: Jackson Turner Main, *The Anti-Federalists: Critics of the Constitution 1781–1788* (New York: W. W. Norton & Co., 1974), 171.

65   *it can hardly be argued that [the opponents of the Constitution] were simply "selfish, parochial, ignorant or unscrupulous"*: Ketcham, *James Madison*, 236.

66   *"I believe that all men are by nature equally free & independent"*: Historical Archives, Education Department Research Files, Gunston Hall Plantation, Lorton, Virginia.

67   *That was how they had run Virginia, and it is surely how they must have viewed the matter of running the country:* Lewis B. Wright, *Cultural Life in the American Colonies* (New York: Harper & Row, 1957), 5.

67   *"The youthful Washington . . . longed to be part of the fashionable society":* Richard Norton Smith, *Patriarch: George Washington and the New American Nation* (Boston: Houghton Mifflin, 1993), 5.

70   *Letters . . . poured in to Mount Vernon, reminding him that there was no possible alternative to his becoming president:* Freeman, *Washington,* 555.

71   *"You had prepared me to entertain a favorable opinion of General Washington, but":* Abigail Adams, quoted ibid., 231.

71   *[Washington] was imbued with such values of the old Romans as self-possession and civic honor:* Marcus Cunliffe, *George Washington, Man and Movement* (New York: Mentor Books, 1955), 156.

72   *"The proofs you have given of your patriotism and of your readiness to sacrifice":* Quoted in Freeman, *Washington,* 560.

72   *"Sir, I have been long accustomed to entertain so great a respect for the opinion of my fellow-citizens":* Quoted ibid.

72   *". . . as the Constitution of the United States, and the laws made under it, must mark the line of my official conduct":* Quoted ibid., 573.

74   *"How unfortunate . . . that internal dissensions should be harrowing and tearing our vitals":* Washington, quoted ibid., 608.

75   *"It is no more that tolerance is spoken of":* Quoted ibid., 585.

77   *"Your being at the helm, will be more than an answer to every argument":* Jefferson, quoted ibid., 606.

79   *"I . . . have no motive to consult but my own inclination":* Smith, *Patriarch,* 136.

79   *"Those who knew Jay best knew better":* Ibid.

81   *In the end, the luster of all the major players was dimmed during this period:* Ibid., 233.

81   *"[The document] bears hard on the Executive":* Jefferson, quoted in Freeman, *Washington,* 689.

82   *"I am sorry to give you . . . trouble on such a trifling occasion":* Quoted in Fritz Hirschfeld, *George Washington and Slavery* (Columbia, Mo.: University of Missouri Press, 1997), 113.

82   *Mr. Nice Guy disappeared, and Washington . . . replied angrily:* Ibid., 115.

83   *He believed in treating slaves decently:* Ibid., 43.

83   *His intellect, his wisdom, and even his honesty were questioned in hostile editorials:* Freeman, *Washington,* 690.

84   *The farewell is pure Washington:* Ibid., 702.

85   *After many farewell tributes, salutes, and parties honoring President Washington, the first transfer of American presidential power from one human being to another occurred on March 4, 1797:* Ibid., 708.

85   *Washington put concrete around the two-term precedent he had already established:* Ibid., 739.

4. Is a Nigger a Human Being?

90   *"At last we came in sight of the island of Barbadoes":* "The Life of Gustavus Vassa," in Henry Louis Gates, Jr., ed., *The Classic Slave Narratives* (New York: Mentor Books/New American Library, 1987), 37.

93   *[slave gatherings] for funerals and other purposes . . . were thenceforth suppressed:* Allan Kullikoff, *Tobacco and Slaves: The Development of Southern Cultures in the Chesapeake, 1680–1800* (Williamsburg, Va.: Institute of Early American History and Culture, 1986), 329.

95   *"was servin' gal fo' Missus":* Susan Broaddus quoted in Workers of the Writers' Program of the Works Project Administration in the State of Virginia, *The Negro in Virginia* (Winston-Salem, N.C.: John F. Blair, Publisher, 1994), 48.

95   *"I was very much affrighted at some things I saw":* "The Life of Gustavus Vassa," 39.

97   *"An Act about the casuall killings of slaves":* Reproduced in A. Leon Higgenbotham, Jr., *In the Matter of Color: Race and the American Legal Process: The Colonial Period* (London: Oxford University Press, 1978), 36.

100 *The reigning arbiters of this dispute were Jefferson's admiring white biographers:* Annette Gordon-Reed, *Thomas Jefferson and Sally Hemings: An American Controversy* (Charlottesville, Va.: University Press of Virginia, 1997), 195.

102 *white men could usually use their power to take slave women with impunity:* Mechal Sobel, *The World They Made Together: Black and White Values in Eighteenth-Century Virginia* (Princeton, N.J.: Princeton University Press, 1987), 149.

103 *"Oh I was loth, loth to go back":* "The History of Mary Prince," in Gates, *The Classic Slave Narratives,* 197.

104 *"I was soon surrounded by strange men":* Ibid., 190.

106 *"'The custom of the country is such,' wrote a Baptist minister":* Kullikoff, *Tobacco and Slaves,* 382.

107 *Blacks heard the cry of freedom:* Philip S. Foner, *Blacks in the American Revolution* (Westport, Conn.: Greenwood Press, 1975), 25.

2

107   *Some fought at Lexington and Concord:* Benjamin Quarles, *The Negro in the Making of America* (New York: Collier Books, 1987), 46.

107   *Still others acted as scouts and spies:* Sidney Kaplan and Emma Nogrady Kaplan, *The Black Presence in the Era of the American Revolution* (Amherst, Mass.: The University of Massachusetts Press, 1989), 59.

108   *the court agreed with Freeman and ruled that the new constitution had indeed abolished slavery in the commonwealth of Massachusetts:* Ibid., 245.

108   *a "practical refutation of the imagined superiority of our race to hers":* Quoted ibid., 246.

110   *"the opening sentence of [the society's] Articles of Association had the feeling of a great beginning":* Ibid., 100.

111   *"Our neighbors, seeing that our master indulged us":* Quoted ibid., 97.

5. A Blood American

116   *"I was not born in Mississippi, but my story begins there":* Roy Wilkins, *Standing Fast: The Autobiography of Roy Wilkins* (New York: Da Capo Press, 1982), 1.

119   *"Uncle Asberry . . . you better get that boy Willie out of town. . . . He's heading for a lynching, sure":* Quoted ibid., 16.

133   *Madison . . . argued that the Malthusian population dilemma could be solved by European immigration and settlement in the West:* Ralph Ketcham, *James Madison* (Charlottesville, Va.: University Press of Virginia, 1990), 328.

135   *Jefferson's passions led him to excess as well as brilliance:* Merril D. Peterson, *Thomas Jefferson and the New Nation* (London: Oxford University Press, 1970), 359.

137   *"Every thinking honest man rejects it [slavery] in Speculation, how few in practice?":* Patrick Henry quoted in Workers of the Writers' Program of the Works Project Administration in the State of Virginia, *The Negro in Virginia* (Winston-Salem, N.C.: John E. Blair, Publisher, 1994), 41.

139   *"What to the American slave is your Fourth of July?":* Frederick Douglass quoted in Richard Kluger, *Simple Justice* (New York: Vintage Books, 1977), 37.

143   *"the prevalence of that pacific and friendly disposition among the people of the United States which will induce them to forget their local prejudices and policies":* Quoted in Douglas Southall Freeman, *Washington* (New York: Collier Books/Macmillan, 1968), 503.

ACKNOWLEDGMENTS

Even a book as slim as this one requires the help and forbearance of many people. My indebtedness runs first to those who over the last few years have had to live with my absorption with eighteenth-century Virginians and with my eccentric work habits and nonexistent filing system: my wife, Patricia King, and our daughter, Elizabeth Wilkins. The impulse to write this book would never have matured had it not been for my acceptance into the community of scholars at George Mason University. My thanks, then, to George Johnson, the late David King, Josephine Pacheco, Marian Deshmuke, Steven Diner, Jack Censer, David Potter, all of my colleagues who are Robinson Professors, and also to President Alan Merton and the person who makes my academic life possible, Iris Knell.

The staffs at George Mason's home, Gunston Hall, and Thomas Jefferson's Monticello have been very helpful. Lucia Stanton at Monticello and Linda Hartman at Gunston Hall have been particularly generous to me. William McFeely and Anette Gordon-Reed have rendered invaluable judgment and advice.

Finally, the support, guidance, patience, and faith of my publisher, Beacon Press, have made this book possible. Deanne Urmy, who first thought this project was worthwhile, has been a good and supportive friend. And then there is my editor, Tisha Hooks, my lighthearted tormentor who committed elegant savagery upon my manuscript, without whose will, talent, and faith this book would never have been completed, and to whom I owe everlasting gratitude.

INDEX